EAT PRAY HUSTLE

DREAM CHASING
GOD'S WAY

A BIBLE STUDY BY

H HAVILAH CUNNINGTON

About the Author   4
Preface   6
Process of a Dream   9

WEEK ONE: DREAM LIFE   10
DAY 1 — Made To Dream: Foundational   12
DAY 2 — For The Sake of It: Missional   16
DAY 3 — You Can't Make It: Inspirational   20
DAY 4 — You Can't Shake It: Gravitational   24
DAY 5 — You'll Wake Up For It: Motivational   28

WEEK 2: DREAM REVEALED   32
DAY 6 — Dreams Revealed: Encounter   34
DAY 7 — Dreams Revealed: Pain   38
DAY 8 — Dreams Revealed: Talent   42
DAY 9 — Dreams Revealed: Covenant   46
DAY 10 — Dreams Stewarded: Momentum   52

WEEK 3: DREAM DEATH   56
DAY 11 — Taken Dreams   58
DAY 12 — Dreams Slipping Away   62
DAY 13 — Running Out Of Time   66
DAY 14 — Shortcutting The Dream   70
DAY 15 — Delaying The Dream   74

WEEK 4: DREAM FULFILLED   78
DAY 16 — Birthing A Dream   80
DAY 17 — Protecting The Dream   84
DAY 18 — Dream Chasers   88
DAY 19 — Authenticating A Dream   92
DAY 20 — Eat. Pray. Hustle. Repeat.   96

HAVILAH CUNNINGTON

I always knew God had a plan for others' lives but never felt God could use me. I struggled with learning disabilities throughout my school years, which caused me to have great insecurity about my value and worth. It wasn't until the age of 17, as I was sitting in a car with friends on my way to a party when I heard the voice of God speak to my heart, "There is more to life than this! I have called you. Come follow me." I spoke out in that moment, telling those in the car that I had a call on my life and they were welcome to come with me, but I was going to serve God.

I remember walking into our house when I got home, kneeling by my bed and saying these simple words, "God, I'm not much. I'm young, I'm a girl with no special gifting. But if You can use anyone, You can use me." Now, thinking back to that day, it makes me laugh how I'd hoped the heavens would have opened up, with angels descending and ascending on a heavenly ladder – that didn't happen and I didn't need it to. God heard my cry and He was at work to accomplish His perfect will in my life.

By 19, my twin sister Deborah and I were traveling all over California preaching, teaching and singing at any place that would have us. By 21, we had been in seven different states and Mexico teaching about Jesus and His great plan for this generation!

Now, almost two decades later, I still believe today is the Church's finest hour; if we choose to live with passion, purpose and walk in power. I'm passionate about seeing individuals encounter God in a real way and seek to blow the lid off common misconceptions, personal limitations, and powerless living. My heart and passion is to inspire and challenge others to become all God has designed them to be.

Today I wear many hats: wife, mom, pastor, teacher, daughter and friend. My husband Ben and I were leaders at The Rock of Roseville Church for the past 15 years but made a huge transition by moving to Redding, California, to be the Directors of Moral Revolution. Two years ago, we put my first Bible study online to inspire those who followed our travels and ministry. Welcomed with tremendous warmth, it encouraged us to continue providing daily devotionals. Now over 20,000 people have joined our studies from all over the world. Eat. Pray. Hustle. is our fourth Bible study.

Most days, you can find us doing something to wrangle the energy of our four young sons: Judah, Hudson, Grayson, and Beckham. We love the outdoors, eating good food, being with friends, and exploring someplace new. We love family and are building ours one day at a time.

PREFACE

It was another Sunday, and we had all migrated to Whiskeytown Lake for an afternoon meal. It was becoming more of a routine as the summer months went on and the heat was getting harder to outrun. We were a lively group. There was no formal invite, just so and so brought so and so; a simple, "I'll invite them!" and we gathered.

With almost 20 kids in tow and half as many adults, we were like a small church. When you have a group of parents who understand what it's like to have a large family, there's almost an ease that hits the group, things get simple, conversations get started, and you begin to relax in the moment.

I loved what was happening. I had been in similar communities, and friendships. There's a particular chemistry that you can't put your finger on, but it starts feeling like family … it's good for the soul.

Unbeknownst to each of us, we were on very similar journeys. Even though our daily lives might look like fraternal twins, we were twinning (I'm an actual twin, so I feel like it's ok to use this word… wink) on the inside. We had an undercurrent running deep, and it was traveling in the same direction.

Let me explain…

One of the friends has five children. They travel the world as missionaries for a good portion of the year; chasing a dream they had to ignite a redemptive story that would start in our very own country. The dream begins with a sustainable piece of land to grow a children's village and family home; eventually building a farmland property to house kids from the foster care system, single moms, and the orphan. It would be a working farm with sustainable resources, giving those living on the property a place to recover, renew, and rebuild.

One of the families is chasing the dream to become counselors and coaches to those around them. Fighting negative family history, one relationship at a time. They are building a community they never had and chasing the dream of intimacy in relationship with each other and with others.

Another friend just bought numerous amount of acreage outside of town. They gave up their regular home to live in an RV on the land, with their five kids. They are chasing a dream to live debt-free but also build a house on the property. Their enormous idea is to start a program to help train missionaries to go overseas with proper anti-kidnapping skills. With her husband's highly skilled and classified background, he will use this gift, along with her unique gifts, to build this dream; creating a place to develop and train individuals going to the nations from their backyard.

Another couple has a beautiful story of restoration and redemption. They're dreaming about restoring the lives of others. They're kicking fear in the face and journeying ahead into the unknown. As they hold on to the promise that all things work together for good, they are quickly seeing it before their eyes. He loves to work with his hands outside, nurturing the land. She loves to work within the family, nurturing the home. They are partnering, building their dream, on a ranch and heading up a restoration ministry. And in the middle of all this dreaming, God deposited the dream of having another baby. After all these years, it was a dream revealed, and a dream come true.

A friend and her husband moved up from LA having become successful screenwriters and directors in the industry for many years. They left the LA vibe to find a place of refuge and a place to build their family. Their dream chasing resulted in them buying an old 1800's style farmhouse on some picturesque land. They realized their dream was to write stories and empower the industry from this place of peace. They believe the quality of life will bring out the quality in the stories they tell.

I'm not a master of the obvious, but I did have a moment of clarity, as I sat back and smiled (OK ... I cried like a baby). I was thinking about each of these powerful friends and the way they live their lives. Honestly, it's their sheer determination and gut-wrenching courage and just plain crazy dream chasing that leaves me breathless. On paper, it's madness. It doesn't add up but that's all a part of pursuing the promise. It's the process of a dream and it's the only way we build the life we want to live.

Chasing dreams is part of life if you want a good life. It's part of the hustle. It's part of the God-induced DNA, which requires us to forge ahead into the unknown; believing there is more out there for us beyond what we can see. And this is what I love about each of their lives. Dream chasing won't look the same on all of us but it has the same components. There are no fast tracks to following the promise, but there are things that can significantly help you.

This whole study is about overcoming obstacles, it's about seeing what we can't see, it's about breaking up with focusing on our lack, and plunging into the promises of God. Sometimes it's as simple as a routine of EAT. PRAY. HUSTLE. REPEAT.

Havilah

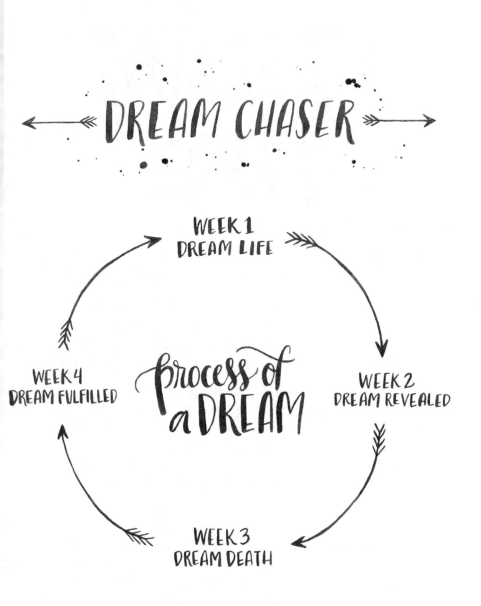

DREAM CHASER

WEEK 1
DREAM LIFE

process of a DREAM

WEEK 2
DREAM REVEALED

WEEK 3
DREAM DEATH

WEEK 4
DREAM FULFILLED

DREAM LIFE

I was hurrying to get ready that morning, pressing play on my phone's Bible reading plan. The goal was to multitask and listen as I went. This seemed to be the easiest way to get Scripture in my life before I began my day with four sons in tow. The book of Romans felt like a great place to start. I was ready for some meaty, get to the point, Apostle Paul goodness. The narrative voice trailed off as I quickly applied my second coat of mascara.

As he read Romans chapter 4, I quickly grabbed my phone scrambling for the repeat button. I needed to listen to this passage again. For some reason, the words coming out of the little speaker felt like they were being spoken right to me. As if Paul was looking at me straight in the eyes, grabbing me by the lapels of my spiritual shirt, and shaking each and every word straight into my heart and soul.

I heard the story of Abraham. No... I mean I really heard the story of Abraham. I heard my story in his story. Have you ever had that happen? You read something, or you see something, and all of the sudden you see yourself in that exact time and place. I began to see Abraham. I saw his divine faith. I saw his "crazy" hanging out. He was a man of God but not a religious man. He made mistakes, but he was trying. He had a dream, a vision, that haunted him every time the night sky lit up with stars. It was always in his face. I'm sure it was amazing, and I'm sure it was terrifying.

Abraham was a man just like us, and he was hustling. What do I mean by that? He had a dream deposited in him as a seed, and he was doing everything he could to help it grow. But the vision required that he do the first thing in front of him without looking around wondering if it was the right thing. He was eating, praying, and hustling most days ... just like many of us!

This whole study is designed to help you understand the attributes of a God Dream. We will uncover what a Dream Chaser looks like and the signs of your greatest dreams revealed. One of the weeks we will expose what Dream Killers look like and what we can do to stay protected. We will learn to nurture the dream, care for it and live it out. I seriously can't wait to jump into the study with you. So, my fellow dream chaser, grab your seat belt and buckle up... We have nothing to lose but heaven!

ROMANS 4:17-25 (MSG)

We call Abraham "father" not because he got God's attention by living like a saint, but because God made something out of Abraham when he was a nobody. Isn't that what we've always read in Scripture: God saying to Abraham, "I set you up as father of many peoples"? Abraham was first named "father" and then became a father because he dared to trust God to do what only God could do: raise the dead to life; with a word make something out of nothing. When everything was hopeless, Abraham believed anyway, deciding to live not on the basis of what he saw he couldn't do but on what God said he would do. And so he was made father of a multitude of peoples. God himself said to him, "You're going to have a big family, Abraham!"

Abraham didn't focus on his own impotence and say, "It's hopeless. This hundred-year-old body could never father a child." Nor did he survey Sarah's decades of infertility and give up. He didn't tiptoe around God's promise asking cautiously skeptical questions. He plunged into the promise and came up strong, ready for God, sure that God would make good on what He had said.

MADE TO DREAM:
FOUNDATIONAL

Storyline — *God had a unique plan and purpose for Abram on earth. He gave Abram a dream to initiate partnership and inspire him to live out his purpose.*

GOD HAS A UNIQUE PURPOSE FOR YOUR LIFE

Your life is very important to God. Have you ever thought about how vital you are to this earth? What could God accomplish through your story? Everything God has done and everything He will do comes directly from the life of a man or woman. He will use a life just like ours to display His reality to our world. In fact, that's how He designed His whole kingdom. Each of us has a vital role, none more important than another, but each working together. God has a unique plan and purpose for your life just as Jesus did when He walked the earth.

DREAMS INITIATE PARTNERSHIP

When Jesus left Earth and returned to Heaven, He gave us a promise. He promised he would go to the Father, but said it was better because He would send one the same as Him in Spirit to come to earth. He was talking about the Holy Spirit. He wants each of us to be filled with His Spirit.

JOHN 14:26 (NIV)

But the Advocate, the Holy Spirit, whom the Father will send in My name, will teach you all things and will remind you of everything I have said to you.

Instead of Jesus walking on the earth as one man fully God, the Spirit would fill each of us, and God would fill the earth. Not that we would become God's, but we would become conduits through whom God could bring the Kingdom of heaven to earth. We would participate and partner with God. Seeping into every aspect of culture, family, and generations until the whole earth understands and knows about the one true God.

And this is why your life is so important. The dreams that you dream are invaluable. Your life is the origin for the whole world knowing about God. Did you ever stop to think that maybe your dreams are God dreams? The dreams in your heart are the very birthplace for supernatural realities.

DREAMS INSPIRE US TO LIVE OUT OUR PURPOSE

In this study, we will follow the life of Abraham and Sarah in the Bible. You will become very familiar with their lives. We will see what it took for them to become Dream Chasers. The Dream was pivotal to keeping them moving forward, and we are no different. God storylines our life through dreams because if He showed us the whole thing in real time we would get overwhelmed with details and nuances. Our minds can hold stories far more than they can hold data. So God designed our minds to dream dreams with Him. To storyline with the Holy Spirit. To imagine impossible ways to reach the world, dig ourselves out of the darkest pits, and live the redemptive moments we've only imagined.

This is why the Prophet Joel said,

Joel 2:28 (NIV)
"And afterward, I will pour out my Spirit on all people.
Your sons and daughters will prophesy,
your old men will dream dreams,
your young men will see visions."

If we look inside each of us, there is a sincere desire to help the world around us. We don't want to live our lives in vain, wasting our life. We may chase after money, popularity, independence, intellect, power, prestige, experience, ministry, family, etc., but within the journey there is a holistic cry that comes out of every human soul that says, "I want to know my life touched the world around me. I want to know I left the world a better place. It wasn't all about me, and I contributed to a picture bigger than my own."

The dreams in our hearts will often encompass a way to reach the world greatly. They will be crazy! You may sit at times, and your brain will wander and daydream. God can use your fantasies, your imagination, and your thoughts to reach the world around you in powerful ways. We just have to listen and see what Holy Spirit is speaking.

WITHOUT A DREAM, YOU WON'T LIVE PURPOSEFULLY

Dreams inspire us to live out our purpose. Without a dream, you won't live purposefully. The Bible is very clear that without a purpose we will perish.

Proverbs 29:18 (KJV)
"Where there is no vision, the people perish:"

If you lack hope, it's because you lack vision. If you lack purpose, it's because you don't have a dream. Don't get stuck! This study is designed to help you move forward and find the dream in your heart. I believe you're going to have a breakthrough because you're hungry for a breakthrough. God is the one who gives us hunger and what He initiates, He always rewards.

MAIN THOUGHTS TODAY

- God has a unique purpose and plan for your life
- Dreams initiate partnership
- Dreams inspire us to live out our purpose
- Without a dream, you won't live purposefully

ADD FIVE MINUTES TO YOUR STUDY
TODAY, I WANT YOU TO CONSIDER THE TRUTH THAT YOU WERE MADE TO DREAM. YOU WERE MADE TO HAVE A VISION AND PURPOSE FOR YOUR LIFE.

Do you believe God could use you to reach your world? Ask yourself if there are any obstacles in your mind that would cause you to question this.

Because God initiates relationship through dreams, have you invited* Holy Spirit to come live inside of you? If so, do you find it easy to partner with Him in your life? What are some of the hindrances?

Do you struggle feeling purposeless in life? Maybe in one area: Marriage, finances, community, parenting, ministry, etc. If so, write out a prayer asking God to help you in that one area. Be brave and write down exactly where you need to dream again in your life.

*Inviting Holy Spirit to live inside of you is one of the easiest and most powerful ways to live. The Bible says we need two things to make this happen. We need to believe, and we need to ask. You can do that right where you are. Pray, "Holy Spirit, I believe you are real. Jesus said you would come to Earth in His place to help me live this life. I ask you to come live inside of me. Fill me from the inside out. I receive your power today!"

WRITE OUT YOUR PRAYER HERE (OR IN YOUR JOURNAL)

FOR THE SAKE OF IT
MISSIONAL

Storyline — *The dream was much bigger than Abram having a baby. We were in the lineage of that dream!*

DREAMS KEEP US MOVING FORWARD

The Bible says, "Without a vision, you will perish." (see Proverbs 29:18) Having a dream for your life is vital to your ability to thrive and make a difference on this earth. Dreams are the equalizer. Dreams are the motivators. Dreams are the communicators. Dreams keep us moving forward, believing there is still more in this life for us. They are God's language to us. Abram received a dream from God. We see God taking him out to the night sky and showing him a galaxy of stars, telling him to look up. Explaining to him, "These will be your descendants. As far as you can see." We can imagine how overcome Abram was. A child meant abundance, lineage, legacy, and promise. More than anything, God had initiated this dream. It was beautiful, vivid, wild, and breathtaking.

DREAMS GET YOU IN ON THE BIG DREAM

Even with this glorious moment, there was more than met the eye for Abram. Abram saw a son in his near future. Abram saw his inheritance and his abundance. But deep in the sky as Abram saw his children, God too saw his very own children. When God gives you a dream, you always get in on the bigger dream. Abram had no idea this verse would be written about him thousands of years later.

Matthew 1:1
"This is the genealogy of Jesus the Messiah, the son of David, the son of Abraham:"

His name and the name of Jesus would be in the same family genealogy. His children would be direct descendants to our story and the story of our Redeemer. Abram could never have known God's dream contained his dream. God was pushing all of heaven to make this a reality.

FOR THE WORLD, GOD DID EVERYTHING
"For God so loved the world that he gave his one and only Son, that whoever believes in him shall not perish but have eternal life."
John 3:16 (NIV)

It's important to understand God deeply and unapologetically loves the world. He would do anything for her, and He has. I know we can hear this often and possibly miss how foundational this is to everything He does. God is always going in one direction. He is rescuing the world with His love, and He's inviting us in on the movement. Don't be that surprised your dream is directly connected to showing the world the love of God in a practical way. It's what He's been doing from the very beginning. He said very clearly in the book of Matthew, "You are the salt of the earth... the light of the world... let your light shine before men." (See Matthew 5:13-16)

Because our dream is a part of His dream and our mission is a part of His grand mission, we will live Missional lives. Simply, when we live as Dream Chasers, it changes the way we do life. Everything we do from here out points in one direction. We are people on a mission to fulfill the Great Commission.

MISSIONAL LIVING REQUIRES SACRIFICE
Dreams begin lifetime journeys with God. They will take us to places we've never imagined and to people we've never considered. Abram had to do this very thing. He had to leave his homeland. He was required to wait for the promise of the

dream. It didn't just come to him one day; he had to go on a journey with God. Much of the voyage required sacrifice and trust. Many people want to dream with God, but they don't want to sacrifice for the dream. It's impossible to have anything worth having unless you have worked, believed, prayed, hoped, and truly sacrificed to possess it.

God is always going in one direction. He has one mission, yet he doesn't mind using many ways to get there. He's big enough to use the smallest things as conduits for the greater good.

MAIN THOUGHTS TODAY

- Dreams keep us moving forward
- Dreams get you in on the BIG Dream
- For the world, God did everything
- Missional living requires sacrifice

ADD FIVE MINUTES TO YOUR STUDY

TODAY, I WANT YOU TO CONSIDER THE MISSION OF THE DREAM. YOU ARE NOT ALONE, AND YOUR PURPOSE IS CONNECTED TO THE ULTIMATE PLAN OF GOD.

What dreams in your life keep you motivated and moving forward?

The dream of being a wife and a mother.

How is your personal dream connected to God's BIG dream? Is this a new thought? Explain.

Never thought of it to be honest. I dont even know how my dream is connected to God's BIG Dream. Holy Spirit show me.

Living on a mission and chasing dreams God's way will require sacrifice. Have you considered what type of sacrifice you're willing to experience? What area in your life would be the hardest to sacrifice?

Sacrificing My dream of having a family would be hard; My parents (Mom) and sister; My mentor

WRITE OUT YOUR PRAYER HERE (OR IN YOUR JOURNAL)

Lord, help me to be motivated by dreams. Give me dreams. Help me to see how they connect to Your BIG dream.

YOU CAN'T MAKE IT

INSPIRATIONAL

Storyline — *God initiates the dream, and it's always more than we can imagine. He's the one holding us.*

THE DREAM WILL ALWAYS BE MORE THAN YOU CAN PULL OFF

Abram learned to respect the difference between his ability and God's capacity. He dared to trust God to do what only God could do. This is where the magic happened... otherwise, known as FAITH!

Let me explain.

We have four boys, four sons. Each of our boys have gone through the developmental stages of infancy to little boy stage. There's always a point where they learn to do something, but they're not sure what is their body and what is your body. They may be washing their hands, but you are holding them up to the sink. You may shift your weight, and they panic believing they are going to fall. So what I often would say to them is, "Don't worry! Mommy's got you." What that meant was, "I'm big enough, strong enough and adult enough to see everything that's going on." Pretty soon they confidently run over, "Mama, hold!" and when I swiftly pick them up as they wash, drink, or whatever they like, they don't question if I'm going to be able to hold them or not.

The above analogy is a clear picture of what's happening in Abram's story. Even though God has given him a promise and a beautiful picture of his dream, he still has no ability to make it happen. Each and every time Abram tries to step out on his own, it's as if God holds Abram close saying, "Daddy's got you!"

God will always pull on our abilities (which He gave us) and sprinkle it with 'out of this world' moments. He loves to put His SUPER in our NATURAL. The Holy Spirit is just waiting to do more in and through your life than you could imagine. But even when you try and comprehend what He wants to do, you'll walk away, shaking your head, thinking, "I didn't even know that was possible. Only God could pull this off." It's what He loves to do! Give us dreams bigger than ourselves. Think about Abram, sitting under that starry sky, watching all those stars twinkling at him, being promised a dream as far as the eye could see. I can imagine him laying down on his back in the cool grass looking up with hot tears streaming down his face. He had waited so long. His heart ached for himself and his wife to have even just one child and now he had the promise of a sky full. It's almost more than he could bear. When God shows us a dream, it's meant to inspire faith in us. Getting us to reach higher, run faster, last longer and dream bigger than we've ever dreamt before.

THE DIFFERENCE BETWEEN YOUR ABILITY & GOD'S CAPACITY

Just like Abram, we will feel a little awkward stepping out to believe the things God has for our lives. We may wonder if He's going to drop us or forget He's holding us. That's normal. But the more we learn to walk by faith, the more comfortable we will be in living out our dreams even if we can't see them quite yet.

Let's take a moment and remind ourselves of what faith means. Hebrews Chapter 11, verse 1 gives us the exact meaning. It says, "Now faith is confidence in what we hope for and assurance about what we do not see." (NIV)

I love how the Amplified version describes it, "faith comprehends as fact what cannot be experienced by the physical senses."

It's normal to want to experience God through our physical senses, but that's not faith. Faith is in your belief system. It's like walking up to a chair and sitting down. You have confidence that the chair is going to hold you. You can think about it, talk about it, analyze its construction, but eventually you're going to have to put your weight on it and see if it can hold you. You're going to have to, in faith, sit down and believe. When we choose to live a life of a dream chaser, and honor the vision God has placed in our hearts, we will have to be experts in God's capacity. We will have to know without a doubt what He's capable of and stand on that firm foundation. Having Faith is the main ingredient; without it, the recipe for life just doesn't work.

MAIN THOUGHTS TODAY

- The dream will always be more than you can pull off
- God will always do His part
- There is a difference between your ability and God's capacity

---

ADD FIVE MINUTES TO YOUR STUDY

TODAY I WANT YOU TO CONSIDER THE INSPIRING DREAM OF GOD FOR YOUR LIFE. IT'S BIGGER THAN YOUR CAPACITY, BUT INSTEAD OF DEVELOPING FEAR, LET IT DEVELOP FAITH.

QUESTIONS *(Take time to write in your Journal)*

In what areas have you have been trying to accomplish things that are beyond your capacity?

Is there a better way to trust God in this season?

Have you been talking down to yourself?

What do you think God is saying to and about you?

WRITE OUT YOUR PRAYER HERE (OR IN YOUR JOURNAL)

G O D   D R E A M

Storyline — *The dream seems to wrap its arms around us and not let us go. No matter how far away we are from it, we are still pulled in its direction.*

OUR ORIGINAL STORYLINE

The Bible says, "God created mankind in his own image." (See Genesis 1:27) It also says when we were formed in our mother's womb He was watching our development (Psalm 139:13). Sometimes that reality can seem so out of reach. It's hard to imagine we are so personalized when there are billions of us on this planet. And yet, it only takes one encounter with God to know you've been created to be known and loved by Him.

Even with the understanding that we are loved and known, it's important to know why we are here. Why did God put me here? What's my life suppose to be? Did He just need to fill the earth, so he threw a few more humans down? Not one bit! In fact, it's the exact opposite according to scripture. As we look deeper in Scripture, we find a passage in the New Testament about King David.

Acts 13:36 (NIV)
"Now when David had served God's purpose in his own generation, he fell asleep; he was buried with his ancestors and his body decayed."

This passage gives us understanding that David had a specific time to be on earth, and when it was complete, God took Him. We can be confident God placed us on the earth with a plan and a purpose. You're right on time! It doesn't matter if you weren't planned according to human intentions; it was God's intent. You can ground yourself in that reality. The BIG idea: God knew and created you to be here before He even formed the earth. This is your time!

GET BUSY TRUSTING GOD
The beauty of Abram's story took off at a specific point. He got busy trusting God in what He could do and stopped worrying about what he couldn't. Merely focusing on overcoming doubt can be a distraction to living a lifestyle of trust. If every time I picked up my kids they were constantly trying not to be afraid, their main focus would still be on fear. But if they set their attention on the task at hand, they would be more prone to stay focused on what's in front of them rather than being worried about not falling.

Abraham realized his focus had to be on what God was able to do. He had to be consumed with the reality that God was big enough, strong enough, and mighty enough to make anything, and that everything happens according to His purpose.

Can I be honest? For some of us, it's going to take all our effort not to focus on what we can't do, but on what God can do. We have to break up with our addiction to focusing on weakness. I would go as far as to say that some of us believe it's humility, but we are partnering with weakness. If I saw my boys talk to themselves like we often talk to ourselves, I would be the first to interrupt them. What I see in them is far greater than what they see in themselves: potential, beauty, life, creativity, new beginnings, world changers, history makers, etc.

The point: it's hard for me only to see their limitations without also seeing their massive potential because I love them and I believe in them. This is a small portion of how God honestly feels about you. When you bump up against what God has for you, you will feel hugely inspired. The Holy Spirit will inspire you to believe for huge things; more than you have ever imagined or thought for yourself.

MAIN THOUGHTS TODAY

- Dreams bring us back to our original storyline
- The dream holds the hope
- Get busy trusting God

ADD FIVE MINUTES TO YOUR STUDY

TODAY I WANT YOU TO MEDITATE ON GOD'S DESIRE TO HAVE YOU HERE ON THIS EARTH IN THIS GENERATION. TAKE SOME TIME TO GROUND YOURSELF IN THIS REALITY.

Have you considered God's placement of your life in this generation? How does that make you feel?

If you are still on the earth, then you still have purpose and time to fulfill God's dream for your life. What are some ways you can let go of regrets and move forward?

Do you live a life that points to trusting God? What is something you can do today to show you trust Him with your story?

WRITE OUT YOUR PRAYER HERE (OR IN YOUR JOURNAL)

YOU'LL WAKE UP FOR IT
GRAVITATIONAL

Storyline — *You'll WAKE up for it. If given an opportunity, you would get up every morning just to do it. It wouldn't be about paying the bills or climbing a career ladder. You'd do it because it's in your heart. It would be the great motivator!*

Today, I want you to take some time and ask the Lord to begin to awaken your heart toward the God dreams He's placed inside of you. Even if you don't know what they are, that's okay. We're going to learn a lot about that this week.

GOD WILL ALWAYS DO HIS PART

Even though the dream lives in you, you must remember God is the One who places it there. He is more invested in the dream than you are. I'm always reminded what it's like with my boys. Each time I think about them succeeding; living whole lives physically, mentally, emotionally, and most importantly spiritually, I burst with love and joy. I'm FULLY invested! I can't help but want them to live in the fullness as God intended. I'm a part of the dream as much as they are … if not more. This is a small example of how God feels and thinks about us. He is FULLY invested in us. He wants to see us living our lives in wholeness. The dream He had in His heart long ago for each of us personally could be carried not just to fulfill our lives but to achieve His eternal purpose.

God's investment leads us to understand He has a part to play in the dream. He loves to participate because He loves the relationship it brings. He loves to talk to us about it. He doesn't tire of our heart or the things we hope are to come. Instead, He longs to have the relational connection. God wants to sit and dream with us. He wants to show us starry nights and watch us gasp in disbelief. He loves the lifelong journey, the mountains and valleys, the white-knuckle rides and the tear-stained face. He laughs with our belly laughs and engages in our exhausted lapse after a good run. He's in it for the journey and in it for the dream. Just like my boys reaching out their hands, we will need to, in confident faith, say to Heaven, "Daddy, I'm ready to try again!" The more we lean on His strength, His ability to take our inability, it will allow us to do some incredible things. And just like we don't shame our kids for trying something when they're little, he's not shaming us when we're trying to learn or do something new, like learning to walk by faith.

Start by praying this prayer and speaking this confession out loud. Remember, He hears every word you say. When you confess with your mouth and believe in your heart, the Bible says, the work has already begun.

DREAMS HOLD RELATIONSHIP

I would suggest that God loved the journey Abram was on with Him. God could have had Sarai pregnant the next day, but instead He lived in relationship with Abram. He was teaching Him more than a promise fulfilled. God was showing Abram what it takes to make a Father. He doesn't give up. He deals with his issues. He trusts God. These lessons are not "one-night stand" lessons. It's a covenant relationship, in-it-for-life type of life. God was invested in the nightly stargazing, heart to heart, relationship that Abram was working out because he was called a Father to many.

MAIN THOUGHTS TODAY
- God will always do His part
- Dreams hold relationship

ADD FIVE MINUTES TO YOUR STUDY
TODAY IS ALL ABOUT THE INTERNAL PULL OF THE DREAM OF GOD
FOR YOUR LIFE. CONSIDER HOW MUCH GOD IS INVESTED IN YOU
PERSONALLY.

"What would you wake up for?" or "What do you do just because you enjoy it, not for any monetary gain?"

Becoming a Dream Chaser is learning to live in a constant relationship with Holy Spirit. Do you live like a "One Night Stand" or a "Married for Life" partner?

What areas of our study this week spoke to you the most? Explain.

- Made To Dream: Foundational
- For The Sake of It: Missional
- You Can't Make It: Inspirational
- You Can't Shake It: Gravitational
- You'll Wake Up For It: Motivational

WRITE OUT YOUR PRAYER HERE (OR IN YOUR JOURNAL)

DREAM REVEALED

Too many of us look for God's dream our whole lives, believing it's like a carrot on a stick, just out of reach. Welcome to being human! But just because it's normal doesn't mean it's right. Dreaming with God shouldn't be a chore. It shouldn't separate the ordinary man from the man who fought battles, clung to promises and tasted sweet victory. It should be the 'right of passage' for all of us. Journey on, finding our personal property, and landing in our Promised Land.

Honestly, it took me a long time to discover what chasing dreams God's way resembled. I was surprised to find it right in front of me. I spent years asking God what His plan was for my life. I remember almost running to church altars asking God for just one word to show me I was on the right track and finally finding my resolve.

No sooner after discovering and displaying God's dream for my life, did I begin to hear from many of you. You wanted to know what God had called you to do, too. Many of you asked for mentorship towards your dreams. You wanted me to share the 'secret sauce' of dreaming with God and seeing it come to pass. My heart ached for you. Not because of something I read, but because of my personal journey. I understand the quest for significance. I understood your desire to be effective in your everyday life. To live as a dreamer, fully engaged in the dream God imagined for you long ago.

I began to consider what I read in the Bible and began to see a pattern to discovering God's vision for your life. I wanted you to see it for yourself! I outlined the four key elements to understanding your particular call and grace. I prayed, asking God to show me if I missed anything. I believe with these key spiritual and very practical elements operating in your life, you will see significant change. You will experience a sovereign momentum just as I have in my life.

These elements are constant reminders for me as well. It's the secret sauce that keeps me in my lane on life's highway and out of other people's lanes. It allows me to have a deep peace, knowing I'm not going to miss the will of God for my life.

As we continue to study the life of Abram and Sarai, consider your life. What elements did Abram, soon to become Abraham, possess in his life? Did Sarai become Sarah because she began to embrace her personal and unique journey with God?

Lastly, take your time this week. Some of this will be very obvious, and some will be new thoughts. If you find yourself becoming discouraged, don't allow yourself to stay there. Push yourself to find the truth. The Bible says the truth will set you free (John 8:32).

I believe us finding the truth about ourselves allows us to be truly free.

John 8:36 (NIV)
"So if the Son sets you free, you will be free indeed."

DREAMS REVEALED
ENCOUNTER

Storyline — *Abram encountered the Lord and received a dream that would last him a lifetime. Many of us will receive a dream through a personal encounter with the Holy Spirit.*

DREAMS COME THROUGH PERSONAL ENCOUNTERS

The Holy Spirit reveals His dreams through encounters. Just like Abram, God will surprise you. He will initiate a sacred moment when He will share His heart with you. You won't be expecting it; in fact, your life may be going in an opposite direction. I could think of countless stories in the Bible where individuals encountered God, and their lives were never the same. The moment alone did not change them, but they left with a dream or a vision of what they were to do and who they were to be from that point on.

Look at the story in the Bible of the woman at the well (See John 4:1-26). She went to the well that day to gather water. She was out during a time when other women in her culture didn't collect water. She didn't go with the other women because she was ashamed of her story. Jesus met her there. He began to prophesy over her. He spoke to her about her life, and her eyes opened to who she was and, more importantly, who Jesus was. After she had spoken with Jesus, she ran into the town, telling everyone about Jesus, saying, "I met a man who told me everything about my life." She left with more than just an encounter. She ran off with the dream of how He saw her and hope for her future.

Look at the apostle Paul, a hater and a killer of Christians (see Acts 9:1-19). He was journeying on the road to Damascus. At once the Spirit of God interrupted his journey and spoke with him, blinding him. At that moment everything changed! After he had encountered the Spirit of God, his life was changed, and he received a message for the world. He wrote over two-thirds of the New Testament, and it all came from an encounter.

Ask yourself what encounter you've received from God or if God has spoken to clearly to you in your life. One thing that has helped me enormously to see the guiding hands of God in my whole life's timeline, is breaking my life up in seven-year increments and seeing if He spoke to me or encountered me. Take the first seven years of your life. Ask yourself the question, "Did I know God in the first seven years of my life? Did I experience anything significant that gave me a tangible reality of His presence?" If so write it down. If you don't see anything obvious, take the next seven years. Keep noting when He spoke to you, or touched your life. It may surprise you to see how He had His hand working.

ENCOUNTERS GROUND US IN RELATIONSHIP

Encountering God is vital to our walk with Him. It's the only thing that gets us up close and personal. It immediately grounds and pulls us into a relationship with Him. Because God can seem so grand and invisible, it can leave us thinking, "Why would the God who created the whole universe and who runs the galaxy care about my life?" But encountering His tangible presence pulls us into His personal and intimate connection.

He wants us to be known. God didn't put Adam and Eve in the garden to only check on them once a month to see if they were still alive. The Bible says in the book of Genesis that He walked with them each and every day in the garden. They were in a relationship with Him. He initiated connection because He valued relationship. This is true for you as well. God wants to encounter you to build a relationship with you.

ENCOUNTERS GROUND US IN SUPERNATURAL REALITIES

Experiencing God in a supernatural way only confirms His reality. At once we are brought into the unseen world of the supernatural. Everything we have believed, prayed and hoped becomes evident. We have seen or encountered something far beyond the natural. Many times this encounter happens when we need a miracle. We pray, asking God to reveal another way beyond our abilities. It is at that moment we see God do something only a God could do. It's a miracle! When we witness supernatural miracles, it grounds us in the supernatural. We know if we hadn't seen it with our own eyes we wouldn't believe it. But we did see it, and we can't explain it away. At that moment, we believe in a greater way than ever before. We have become witnesses of God's nature and His capabilities.

ENCOUNTERS BUILD PERSONAL HISTORY

The book of Revelation gives us two ways to defeat the enemy in this world. He says in Revelation 12:11 (NIV)

They triumphed over him by the blood of the Lamb and by the word of their testimony; they did not love their lives so much as to shrink from death.

Your personal testimony is your special power. It's yours, and no one can take it from you. Not only that, it's the evidence of God at work in your life. Each time you talk about what God has done, it adds power to your life and confirms His reality. Don't let the enemy lie to you and tell you, "You don't have a great testimony. It's not that powerful." He knows how powerful your story is, and he's afraid you'll use it.

MAIN THOUGHTS TODAY

- Dreams come through personal encounters
- Encounters ground us in relationship
- Encounters ground us in supernatural realities
- Encounters build personal history

ADD FIVE MINUTES TO YOUR STUDY
TODAY IS ALL ABOUT UNDERSTANDING THE SIGNIFICANCE OF
ENCOUNTERING THE LORD. CONSIDER HOW HE REVEALED HIMSELF
THROUGHOUT YOUR LIFE.

QUESTIONS *(Take time to write in your Journal)*

Do you know the particular times God encountered you
throughout your life?

Have you ever timelined your story?

Take some time to write out a simple timeline in your journal or
on a piece of paper. Add seven-year increments on the timeline.
Ask the Holy Spirit to reveal when and where He made Himself
known during your life. Was someone praying for you? Did you
know there was a God before someone introduced you? Write it
all down.

Is your life set up to encounter the Lord? What specifically are
you doing to create an atmosphere to hear His voice?

WRITE OUT YOUR PRAYER HERE (OR IN YOUR JOURNAL)

DREAMS REVEALED

PAIN

Storyline — *Abram's dream was powerful because of the pain he experienced. Our dreams are personal and connected to our personal pain.*

PROMISE IS REVEALED

God's glory will be revealed in your story of pain and triumph. Sometimes we have to look at the most painful parts of our story to see how God was at work. The times of crisis, heartache, and grief is the place God holds his promise. We don't like it, but it's true.

I remember a very painful moment in my story being diagnosed with Postpartum Depression. I was a young mother, with two littles in our home under the age of two, and I was incredibly overwhelmed. After visiting my doctor and a Christian counselor, I learned I was struggling with a lack of serotonin in my body. Even though I can talk about it now with hope and healing, it was one of the darkest times in my life. The shame I felt for not being a happy, healthy Mom was overwhelming. It took everything I had to get help and begin to dig my way out of an isolating depression. When I was finally standing on my own two legs, the Lord began to speak to me about telling my story. He reminded me that others would find hope and health through my personal experience. It took courage to say, "I was a new Mom, and I was depressed." But I can't count the emails I've received from women all over the world who have experienced similar things. They gained hope from my story. God's dream was to partner with me in the struggle. He wanted to see me free and redeem that moment in time. Not only did I experience

His loving hand lifting me out of the pit, but also He put real tools in my hands to help others. Did I like the fact I went through pain? No. But I can now see how God used it to help others, and it gives me a sense of purpose in the pain.

Remember Abram. He's childless in the world where having children is your claim to fame. He's prayed, cried, struggled, believed, given up and, at that moment, God gives a promise. Abram's pain reveals the promise. It's one thing to believe God for a day but it's entirely different to believe Him for a lifetime. God wanted to use Abram and Sarai's pain. It fortified the hope for their promise, and we gain tools in our struggle. It was not in vain!

DREAMS ARE ROADMAPS TO FREEDOM

We can find ourselves between a rock and a hard place in areas of deep pain or crisis. You don't have to read much of the Israelites' story to understand it's a theme throughout the Bible. You can get stuck in the in-between, crying all the tears you can cry, praying all the prayers you can pray. God will give us a dream in the moment of pain. He won't just rescue us at the moment, but He'll reveal His love and commitment in the pain. The reason God often gives us a promise in the instant is so we don't divorce the pain. He wants us to believe in the moment but also to store up power to help others. The pain you've experienced is not in vain. God desires to use your pain to help others in the same place. It's at the moment we believe God will use everything for those called according to His will (Romans 8:28) that we will find a deep abiding peace. It's important we roadmap our freedom. We need to take the time to understand our process and the road marks we've come to along the way. We will need them to help others.

DREAMS ARE THE POWER OF GOD

Dreams are God's thoughts and purposes revealed in our everyday life. He gives you a supernatural promise of your future. Not just a promise, but hope to accompany the potential. The Bible says in the book of Jeremiah:

Jeremiah 29:11 (NIV)
For I know the plans I have for you," declares the Lord, "plans to prosper you and not to harm you, plans to give you hope and a future."

Every dream God provides us is overflowing with hope. Biblical hope means, "An expectation of God's goodness." Our God dreams position us for God's goodness. The more we walk towards the dream, the more His goodness chases us down. He loves to give His children good gifts. Hope is like a drink of cold water on a dry throat. It's like the promise in the Book of Isaiah.

Isaiah 44:3 (Message)
"For I will pour water on the thirsty ground and send streams coursing through the parched earth."

Hope heals the broken soul. Hope gives new strength to reach out for the promise in the middle of the darkest pain. God's dreams for you are the way out. Dreams are the power of God. It's His thoughts when we lack thoughts, hope when we lack hope, and His reality overriding our seemingly impossible path.

MAIN THOUGHTS TODAY

- Dreams come when a promise is revealed
- Dreams are the roadmap to freedom
- Dreams are the power of God

ADD FIVE MINUTES TO YOUR STUDY

TODAY, TAKE SOME TIME TO ACKNOWLEDGE THE PAIN IN YOUR STORY. LET THE HOLY SPIRIT SPEAK TO YOU ABOUT USING THIS PART OF YOUR STORY TO HELP OTHERS.

If you've never done this before, take a few moments in prayer and ask God where He was in the pain. Ask Him to reveal Himself in a greater way. He may show you a picture of the event, it might just be a feeling of peace, or He may even speak to you about it. If you're struggling with this part, it may be good to look at unforgiveness* that's holding you back.

Here's a Few Things to Help on the Area of Forgiveness:

FORGIVENESS
- Forgiveness does not mean that what they did to you was right
- Forgiveness does not mean that they 'get off scot-free'
- Forgiveness does not mean you give up all your rights

YOUR UNFORGIVENESS
- It does not hurt the one who harmed you
- It hurts only you
- It binds you in a prison of torment
- It often causes you to have bitterness, hatred and anger
- It blocks the fullness of God in your life

EXTENDING FORGIVENESS DOES WONDERFUL THINGS
- You get to step out of the way and let God have a direct line to that person
- It means you are relieved of the burden you have been carrying
- It frees you from a prison of torment
- It closes a door that allowed the enemy to have access to you
- It allows you to say:
  - "I choose to give grace"
  - "I choose to let this person go into God's hands"
  - "I am not going to be their judge"

What promise has God given you in the middle of your pain? How does it link to helping others?

D R E A M S   R E V E A L E D

TALENTS

Storyline — *The plan of God connects you to the gift and grace in your life. Abram was called to be a Father, both physically and spiritually; his dream only confirmed this reality.*

DREAMS CONFIRM WHAT YOU ALREADY POSSESS

There's a fascinating story in the Bible about three men who were gifted talents. Let's read the passage together. (Matthew 25:14-30)

Interestingly, these men were given different amounts of talents. Each of them had a choice to do what they wanted with these gifts. They chose to either 'go for it' and take a risk or bury them in fear. The difference was not in the amount they each received but what they did with it.

Like these men, each of us have received gifts and talents in our lives. God gave them to us before we knew what they were and what to do with them. A talent is something you are naturally good at doing. It doesn't take much to do and with a little effort you can accomplish the task.

My husband loves anything techy. He loves the latest Apple gadgets. Does anyone else live with one of these? (Wink) He's constantly reading up on an upcoming product, applications, and equipment. During our weekly staff meetings, a question will come up about something in that field. We will all turn to him and ask him the question. He usually knows the answer or knows how to find it. It's something that comes easily to him. Is he the best in his field? Does he write the groundbreaking articles? No. But it doesn't negate the fact that he holds an aptitude. It doesn't drain his strength but rather infuses strength. Does this gift carry his whole purpose? No. But it's a great way for him to build the story of God with his natural talents.

Most people miss this in life. They will look at other people and overvalue what they've received, meanwhile undervaluing their personal abilities. The Bible doesn't say 'pastoring or full-time ministry is the most important.' He values the attitude by which we do everything or anything.

The Bible says, in Colossians 3:23 (NIV)

"Whatever you do, work at it with all your heart, as working for the Lord, not for human masters,"

God is interested in using everyone's individual gifts. He wants to take your aptitudes to bless and build His story. It's in the being, not in the doing, that makes all the difference.

DREAMS MAGNIFY YOUR STRENGTH

The dream of God will usually confirm something in your heart. It will coincide with a gift or talent in your life.

Looking at my life, I wasn't a regular speaker but I was a natural-born convincer. I loved to convince my friends and family with my current beliefs. When God gave me a dream to reach my generation, He put within me a desire to communicate. Pulling on my gift to convince, I began to nurture the gift within. I didn't expect myself to become a brain. My first step wasn't to watch YouTube videos of leaders teaching with a Doctorate in Theology. I didn't sit back hoping God would give me a brain or a higher IQ. Instead, I watched videos of leaders with a gift to convince people that the Word was true. I leaned on the way God made me and didn't partner with shame or fear because I didn't have all the tools. God magnified my gift the more I used my talent.

The dream God gives you will partner with your strength. I know we like to use the scripture, "He'll take the foolish things to confound the wise" (1 Corinthians 1:27 NKJV). But when it comes to dream chasing, I like the scripture, "For the gifts and calling of God are without repentance" (Romans 11:29 KJV).

Why would God call you to be a worship leader if you don't sing? God didn't call Sarai to be a Father to the Nations, He called Abraham. Abraham had the entire DNA to be a Dad. He just needed a miracle to make it happen.

DREAMS TEACH YOU STEWARDSHIP

Once you know what your gifts are and the talents God gave you, it's time for serious stewardship. Let's not forget, the man in the story at the beginning of our study didn't have the most talents. He just didn't bury them. If you're always waiting for the perfect time to be who God dreams you to be, you'll never step out. Part of partnering with God is doing your part well and leaving God's part to God. Everything we do is training. Long ago when I began the ministry, I cleaned houses. The dream in my heart was for impact and influence, but I was living a very simple and private life. Instead of resisting what I was doing, Holy Spirit taught me how to steward it. I brought Bible teachings to listen to at the homes I cleaned. I would listen to the Bible read aloud. It was a Bible training school right in the homes of our clients. I look back now and see all the little lessons God was teaching me early on, many of which I still use to this day. Stewarding your gifts is the only way to make them grow and God's dream for your life will always connect to your natural talents.

MAIN THOUGHTS TODAY

- Dreams confirm what you already possess
- Dreams magnify your strength
- Dreams teach you stewardship

ADD FIVE MINUTES TO YOUR STUDY
TODAY, CONSIDER THE GIFTS AND TALENTS GOD HAS GIVEN YOU. FIND WAYS YOU CAN STEWARD WHAT COMES NATURALLY TO YOU.

Do you know the talents God has given you?

Write down five specific gifts on your life. It could be as direct as, "I have a gift to play piano" or "I know how to fix things with my hands." You may be a loyal friend. Acknowledge that grace on your life. The more specific you can be, the better you will see what you can steward well.

Look at these five areas, with the help of the Holy Spirit, and ask Him how you can steward and multiply these talents. Write them down.

Is there an area where you have overvalued some else's gifts and undervalued your own? Take a moment to acknowledge it before God and ask Him to help you value what you have. He would love nothing more than to magnify the gift in your life.

WRITE OUT YOUR PRAYER HERE (OR IN YOUR JOURNAL)

DREAMS REVEALED
COVENANT

Storyline *— Dreams will often come through relationship. Who you are connected with and in covenant with will often reveal your dream. Like Abram, Sarai was just as much a part of the dream as he was.*

DREAMS ARE REVEALED THROUGH COVENANT

I have four sons. One of them has an enormous imagination, and one of them likes to watch his brother dream. Even though he isn't the first one to imagine, he loves to participate in the dream. I like to think of our first son as the "founder" of the dream and the second son as the "carrier" of the dream. What's important is their relationship. The nature to be dreamers is in both of them, and the grandness of the idea expands when both of them pursue it.

When we chase dreams God's way, He will put you in covenant relationships. What does that mean? In the Bible, a covenant was critical. Covenant connected two people together. God would often make promises towards us in the Bible. The way he made contract was through blood. In the Bible, we see Him asking Biblical leaders to take an animal without spot and kill it. The blood was the symbol of relationship and covenant. Covenant makes whatever is available to you, available to me. Think about Jesus dying on the cross. He was an innocent man who shed his blood for us. When one drop of blood shed on the cross, it was enough to break the curse of sin and death. Also making everything Jesus had available to him, available to us. God will often bring us into covenantal relationships.

He wants to expand what's available to us. When a husband and wife marry, they enter into a covenant. What was available to the woman is immediately accessible to the man. God will even bring you into a relationship with leaders in your world. He will call you to become covenant friends. It's a very special relationship and should be entered into seriously.

How does this work towards finding God's dream for your life? You may find yourself as a huge dreamer or often the one who supports the dream. It's the spirit of the dreamer that's the most important, not always the one who gave birth in the beginning. Eventually, the desire takes over, and you both carry it. The origin isn't as important as the dream staying alive. Covenant now makes one person's vision available to the other. When we both carry the dream, it becomes easier to carry. A partnership is always a part of God's story.

Biblically we find this to be true. Mary, the mother of Jesus, was first visited by Holy Spirit. (See Luke 1). She was the first one to receive the dream. She communicated what the Spirit said to her. Joseph, her fiancé, had his struggles but eventually had an encounter himself (See Matthew 1). They both became dreamers, but only Mary was pregnant with Jesus. Mary was the Founder, and Joseph was the Carrier. The Founder and the Carrier are equally as important. What was important was the dream and the reality of Jesus. The origin didn't determine the beauty or the multiplication of the dream. If we look at how big the idea grew from then, we can see we are all carriers now!

Let's go back to the story of Abraham and Sarah. If you remember, Abraham was the one that spoke with God. He was the one that saw the stars in the sky. Eventually, the dream became a reality in Sarah; she was the one who became pregnant. She was the one who carried the lineage of our Christ. We gave birth. But no one will say Abram didn't have a role, or the dream didn't originate with Him. It was a beautiful exchange!

CARRYING THE DREAM IS AS IMPORTANT AS FINDING ONE

What am I trying to say? We need to be careful we don't glamorize the visionary role. Our role may be one who partners with the visionary. One is no more important. You may have a leader, a pastor, a spouse, or a friend impassioned with what God has said. Don't beat yourself up with looking for a dream. God may be calling you to join your dream to theirs. You may be called to carry the idea! Their great dream may become just as much your dream. You may be the place God wants to birth the dream. The gifts and graces in your life are the atmospheres God wishes to use. Just because someone else said it or dreamt it doesn't mean you can't live it. Relax.

PARTNERSHIP IS KINGDOM

I want us to look at one more angle.

God loves and creates the partnership. "No man is an island," someone once said. We are not set up to live out the dream of God in our hearts as islands, as individual notes. God wants us to partner with each other to have a greater sound, a louder voice that echoes through the world. The question is never, "Does God want me to partner?" The question will always be, "Who does God want me to partner with?" So when it comes to dreaming with God, who has God positioned you to dream alongside? Is there someone you can partner with to make the dream happen? These are vital questions. Even God positioned us to partner with his Spirit in a profound way.

It says in 1 Corinthians 3:9 (AMP)

For we are God's fellow workers [His servants working together]; you are God's cultivated field [His garden, His vineyard], God's building.

Another version says we are His co-workers or co-laborers. God has given us the incredible opportunity to work with Him. He will not function without us, and we cannot operate without Him.

When you consider all the ways God could have done His work, it is even more amazing to know He wants our participation. God wants you as His working partner!

Whatever season you're in, whether you are the Originator or the Carrier, whether you're rocking your dream or helping someone else see their dream materialize, it's good to know that God is the original founding dreamer! He would love nothing more than to partner with you to see the dream come alive.

MAIN THOUGHTS TODAY
· Dreams are revealed through covenant
· Carrying a dream is as important as finding one
· Partnership is always kingdom

ADD FIVE MINUTES TO YOUR STUDY
TODAY WE EXPLORED WHAT COVENANT RELATIONSHIPS MAKE AVAILABLE IN OUR LIVES. CONSIDER WHAT COVENANT RELATIONSHIPS YOU ALREADY HAVE AND WHICH ONES GOD MIGHT BE LEADING YOU TO MAKE.

Take a moment to write down the relationships in your life you would consider covenantal. (Don't worry if you don't have any or only a few. This may be a new thought for you, and we never want to rush into partnerships like these.)

What is available in their life that is now available to you?

Would you consider yourself the dreamer or the carrier of the dream? How did today's study help you in this area?

Are there any relationships you feel God leading you towards making a covenant in?

WRITE OUT YOUR PRAYER HERE (OR IN YOUR JOURNAL)

DREAMS STEWARDED
MOMENTUM

Storyline — *The more we invest in our dream through encounter, pain, talent, or covenant, the more we will begin to build momentum. Abram made his dream one day at a time, and we will, too.*

LIVING IN YOUR SWEET SPOT

Living in your sweet spot is living in your Promised Land. Dream chasing isn't just to live in an eternal life of hoping yet never seeing. It's not some 'just out of reach' lifestyle where we never come to a place of fulfillment. We will achieve our promise, and when we do, our whole lives will sync. This isn't to say that everything will be perfect, or we will be perfect. It will be nearly the complete opposite.

ENCOUNTER BUILDS MOMENTUM

Encountering God will consistently build momentum in our lives. Reaching a place of regularly meeting with Holy Spirit changes us. It gives us movement toward His promise. Living in relationship with Him will be your most valuable experience. When we invest time to further encounters and honor those moments, we will gain history with Him. This causes momentum. Momentum could be described as building movement in the same direction while simultaneously building speed and confidence. The Bible says, "The people who know their God shall be strong, and carry out great exploits." (See Daniel 11:32 NKJV)

MOVING THROUGH PAIN BUILDS MOMENTUM

You will begin to understand your pain can have a purpose, and it will no longer hold you paralyzed. The promise we received in our heartbreak will start to sustain us. Hope will rise out of the ashes, and we will be able to see a better day ahead. Using our story of grief will outline helping others. The darkness of the pit won't be the only thing we see. We will be agents of change, using our pain as a powerful weapon against the enemy's schemes. Each time you choose to take your pain and use it to reinforce God's promise, it will be powerful. You will be a vehicle of the breakthrough for those with the same story. It will not be in vain. Each time you focus on the promise and give your pain to God it will build momentum. You will not be stuck, but you will be in movement.

TALENTS BUILDS MOMENTUM

Stewarding the talents and gifts in your life will build incredible momentum. Finding out what God already put in you will push you forward. The key to building strength is to create value. Each time you see the gifts you have, even if they seem small, you invest. There will be more return. Staying on course and valuing what God put in us from the beginning will be very significant. Living in comparison is one of the fastest ways to kill momentum. Don't do it! Fight the desire to be like the men with the talents. Don't hide them. The only way to get them to grow is to keep them out in the open. Growth takes time so be kind to yourself, but keep growing.

COVENANT BUILDS MOMENTUM

A relationship is one of the fastest ways to momentum. God puts people in your life because God knows they carry something you need. Understanding and valuing the right relationships will cause new worlds to open up to you. You can inherit and possess large portions of promise just because you choose to be in a relationship.

My family and I attend a great church. Each week we come we encounter God in a fresh way. The worship is vibrant and skilled, the preaching is revelatory and provoking, and the atmosphere is equally charged and peaceful. We have visitors flock from all over the world just to experience our home church. Can you imagine if I walked in each week and believed that what I'm experiencing is because of me? That would be crazy! Everyone knows we are dipping into the deep pockets of Fathers and Mothers who have gone before us, or those now stewarding their Promised Land. Looking around the room, you see amazing women and men who have given their time, talents and treasures to see this church built. It would be impossible for any of us to experience this atmosphere without covenant.

Our covenant with Jesus made a way for us to enjoy His presence. The covenant our leaders have with their spouses gives us access to their anointing and the agreement fostered in the relationship among friends give us more to experience. Covenant builds momentum in our lives because, frankly, we have more available to us. God loves partnership, and divine partnership is part of God's story.

Dream chasing isn't easy but understanding how to find yours is vital. God reveals His thoughts to you in your encounters with Him. He wants you to discover your promise in your pain, your hidden talents, and to put your gifts on display. He wants to bring you into a covenant relationship, starting with Him. All of these areas hold new found hope and purpose. Don't look any further to chase your dreams God's way. Look for the signs ... they're all around you!

Main Thoughts Today

- Living in your sweet spot
- Encountering builds momentum
- Moving through pain builds momentum
- Stewarding talents will build momentum
- Staying in covenant builds momentum

TODAY WE LOOKED AT LIVING IN YOUR SWEET SPOT AND LEARNING
ABOUT WHAT IT TAKES TO BUILD MOMENTUM IN YOUR LIFE.

QUESTIONS *(Take time to write in your Journal)*

Do you feel like you're living in your sweet spot? Explain.

Have you lacked momentum in your life? What are a few things
you're going to do in the next 24 hours to build momentum?
(Hint: We just looked at four areas this week to help you see
and steward momentum. Making a 'next step' for each of these
areas will help tremendously.)

What areas of our study this week spoke to you the most?
Explain.

- Dreams Revealed: Encounter
- Dreams Revealed: Pain
- Dreams Revealed: Talent
- Dreams Revealed: Covenant
- Dreams Stewarded: Momentum

WRITE OUT YOUR PRAYER HERE (OR IN YOUR JOURNAL)

DREAM DEATH

Even when we have a definite plan for our next step, and we have everything lined up, the dream can still be in jeopardy. Often it's the things we miss that can be the most damaging.

Week three is all about keeping the dream ALIVE! We will expose the dream killers and the things that cause premature birth. To be blunt, no one likes to talk about this reality. You're not going to pop on your favorite worship song or podcast to hear about dead dreams or stillbirth promises. It's not something we like to acknowledge. But the reality in Abraham and Sarah's story is that they made some major mistakes. A crazy turn of events cost them more than they ever anticipated. Let's be honest, it almost cost them the dream. The reality is that many of us have or will experience this part of the story, partly because we were never taught to hold the dream. We didn't know that part of our responsibility is to nurture the vision even when we don't see it. It's not in our nature to invest moments we don't see an immediate return. It was our spiritual parents or even our natural families who missed giving us this information and it caused us a lot of pain and heartache. Some of you live reminded of this every day of your life. Broken promises and distant dreams. It's taken the breath out of you and caused you to live in a survival mode. It's become easier to believe everyone else can chase dreams God's way, but you just seem to miss it every time.

The other half of us know we've done something to kill the dream. We can't put our finger on it, but deep down we struggle with shame and humiliation because the death of our dream is on display. If we had it to do over, we'd do it a thousand different ways. We are stuck in the graveyard of broken dreams, unfulfilled promises and impossible realities.

I believe this week is critical for you. It's the make or break moment when you get to decide if you're a dreamer or a survivor. Are you going to get stuck between the washer and the dryer, the parking lot and the boardroom, the pulpit and the pew, or are you going to rise above? Will you take responsibility for broken down dreams and forgotten promises? God is willing to help you! I implore you to take your time this week and learn. Even if you are chasing your dream and seeing the hand of God move in your life, we are all in danger of these realities. If Abraham and Sarah got swept into the current of these dream killers, then we can too. God is here to aid us in finding remedies, but we have to start by being fully honest.

TAKEN DREAMS

Storyline — *The moment Lot took the land from Abram it seemed as if Lot took a portion of the best part of the Promised Land. Abram trusted the Lord in the conflict even when it felt like part of the dream was taken away.*

DREAMS CAN BE TAKEN

No faster had Abraham believed he was settling into his dream home with his dream life, did it take an immediate turn. Abram's, and his cousin Lot's, shepherds were having a dispute. In fact, it was so bad the two men decided they should part ways. The Bible doesn't tell us much, but something about this quick and immediate decision tells us it must have been pretty bad. Abram chose the way of peace, offering Lot one of two parcels of land.

The Bible says in Genesis 13:10-12 (NIV)

"Lot looked around and saw that the whole plain of the Jordan toward Zoar was well watered, like the garden of the Lord, like the land of Egypt. (This was before the Lord destroyed Sodom and Gomorrah.) So Lot chose for himself the whole plain of the Jordan and set out toward the east. The two men parted company: Abram lived in the land of Canaan while Lot lived among the cities of the plain and pitched his tents near Sodom."

In essence, Lot looked at both properties and saw one was better. It was more watered, like a garden, and it looked like their hometown, Egypt. Abram didn't fight Lot for the land but instead yields to him and settles in Canaan.

I'm sure this was hard for Abram. After all, Lot had followed him to this place. Abram was the one who had the promise. He was the one whom God had promised the land, and now he was dividing it to give the best portion to his cousin, the tagalong.

Have you ever been here before? When you feel like your promise is just about to come into play, someone quickly swoops down and grabs it right in front of you. Maybe you've just had a financial breakthrough, and an unexpected bill comes in. You were given the lead in a department, only to have it taken and split with someone else. Have you waited to be married, found the perfect guy, and now your best friend is marrying him? (Ok, that may be a stretch... but you see where I'm going.)

GOD WILL GET IT BACK

I think we can all learn from the life of Abram at this moment. Abram doesn't panic. He doesn't quickly change his mind and take the land back. He stays true to his word and lets God fight for him. The truth is, if God is going to give it to you then it's His job to keep it for you. The moment we try and hold on to the promise, believing we are responsible for fighting for it, is the moment we lose.

There is a difference between authority and favor in the Bible. We find many men in the Bible that used their power to make something happen. We also see the power of the favor of God. When you have it, it's just a matter of time before you are leading. Consider the story of David and King Saul. Saul was King and had the authority to lead, but David had the favor of God. His favor positioned him to kill Goliath and eventually rule Saul's kingdom. It took time for the authority to be granted to him, but the favor kept him in front of God and man.

So today, if you're struggling with someone having more authority than you and it seems they hold the power of your promise, don't believe that lie. You need the favor of God to rest on you because His favor lasts a lifetime.

CONFLICTS BRING OUT WHAT WE BELIEVE

It's at the moment we feel robbed, taken advantage of, or forgotten, that we find out what we believe. You are not forgotten. You are not a slave. You are a child of God. The enemy will always challenge your identity and ask you why you have a right to be here. If you're not clear on your personal position in God's story, you will feel threatened, powerless, and invisible. It's in knowing we have a God who sees the whole picture and is making all things work together, that we can relax. Grounding ourselves in the reality that no weapon formed against us will prosper will keep hope alive.

Abram could give the land because He had heard the word straight from God. He heard His promise. Sometimes we lack confidence because we only hear secondhand what God is saying about us. We have to go back to the source and ask Him what He thinks. It's in the moment of vulnerability and wondering that we find our answers. Once you've heard it from His mouth, little will stop you.

RIGHT BECAUSE IT'S RIGHT

There's always a point in dream chasing, where we become challenged about what is 'fair' and what is 'right'. I believe there is a big difference according to the Bible. If we are always looking for what is fair, we will live with an attitude of "what's in it for me?" or "you don't deserve it." It's a losing attitude because life doesn't always look fair. We will never know the personal journey of an individual, and we are left only to judge what we can see.

Even Abram didn't stay at the "what is 'fair'?" response. Can you imagine if he had lived with that attitude? How different would things have been? Instead, he did what was 'right'. He looked at how he could resolve the situation and get on with life. Sometimes it's our ability to stop, evaluate, give more than what's fair, and keep going. We have to trust that God will work it out.

Spoiler Alert: Lot's life did not turn out as he had hoped. He thought picking the better land would give him an edge in life. It cost him his reputation, his wife, and eventually the very land he settled on.

MAIN THOUGHTS TODAY

- Dreams can be stolen
- God will get it back
- Conflicts bring out what we believe
- Doing what's right because it's right

ADD FIVE MINUTES TO YOUR STUDY

TODAY WE LEARNED EVEN IF THE DREAM WAS STOLEN FROM YOU, GOD WILL RESTORE IT TO YOU. WE DON'T NEED TO ACT FAIRLY, BUT JUSTLY.

QUESTIONS *(Take time to write in your Journal)*

Is there a dream you have seen taken from you? Did God speak to you about it today? Explain.

What are ways we gain God's favor?

Have you been stuck in your life between being fair and acting just? What is something you're going to do today to help you focus on acting more justly in your life?

WRITE OUT YOUR PRAYER HERE (OR IN YOUR JOURNAL)

THE SLIP AWAY DREAM

Storyline — *Abram goes through a lot of personal hardship. The hardship brings out fear and unbelief in him, resulting in giving Sarai to Pharaoh. Instead of trusting God, Abram tries to solve the problem himself but God cleans it up for him.*

THROUGH SUCCESS AND FAILURE

God gave Abram a promise of a dream. He was to venture into the land of Canaan where God promised meaningful things. He promised to bless him and make him a great nation.

Let's read about it in Genesis 12:1-3

The Lord had said to Abram, "Go from your country, your people and your father's household to the land I will show you. "I will make you into a great nation, and I will bless you; I will make your name great, and you will be a blessing. I will bless those who bless you, and whoever curses you I will curse; and all peoples on earth will be blessed through you."

He was journeying to his Promised Land and his promised life. It's not been easy for him until this point. His Dad died along the way, and his family is following him. I'm sure he felt a bit lost. Just when he thought he might be close, he ventured into a place that held danger. Abram panicked. He told Pharaoh that Sarah was his sister because she was so beautiful that he thought the king might want her as his own. He was afraid he might be killed so he had his wife taken by Pharaoh into his house. But even in the midst of Abram's fear and unbelief, God had a plan.

When Abram didn't know what to do, God did. He had no problem fighting a battle for Abram. We can learn a valuable lesson here. It is the nature of God on display. He knows when we are in over our heads. I can honestly say, there have been times when I'm in way over my head. In fact, if people could hear my thoughts I'd imagine they'd hear something like, "I feel out of control at this moment. I've never done this, and everyone is looking for me to know what to do. Jesus, you can come quickly... how about right now!" Ha! It's true.

The danger wasn't in the fact that Abram had abandoned the plan. The danger was in Abram abandoning the dream. God knew in Abram's heart he wanted to do what God wanted him to, and he just didn't know how.

Part of dream chasing requires us to understand God doesn't have a problem knowing we need Him, we do. I like to say, "God has been God for a long time, and He's excellent at it." God knew just what to do to rescue them. He sent a plague in the middle of Pharaoh's house. When Pharaoh finally put together that Sarai was Abram's wife, he immediately sent her back to him.

GREATEST DREAMKILLERS

The moment Abram bowed down to fear and unbelief was the moment he lost sight of the dream. Ultimately, you can't be looking at two things at once. The Bible says,

"A double minded man is unstable in all his ways."
James 1:8 (KJV)

Truthfully, you can't look at fear and live a brave life. Living an unbelieving life doesn't produce a believing life. No matter how much you plan or prepare, you will be in over your head and the best thing you can do is be aware of the danger lurking around the corner called fear and unbelief. You need a plan! Don't just say, "I've already dealt with it. I'm ok." That's one of the biggest weapons of the enemy in our lives.

Years ago, one of our sons really struggled with getting his hair washed. I don't mean he fought or cried a little. He would scream bloody murder like we were killing him. Each time we went to wash his hair the room would fill with fear. Ben and I would take turns washing because it was a huge ordeal. At one point Ben and I looked at each other and said, "We need a plan!" We were exhausted. We decided to talk with him about fear. We explained to him that he was going to have to fight the fear. We explained that if he would say, "I will not fear" while we were washing his hair he would have something to focus on. We started that night. Judah began to say, "I will not fear." He began to cry as he was saying it. I told him to yell it. If he could use his mouth it would be hard to use his brain for anything else. He began to shout, "I WILL NOT FEAR. I WILL NOT FEAR." The hysteria stopped almost immediately. We continued that pattern until he no longer battled with fear. We had a plan for fear, and fear lost its power. Fear and unbelief are coming to kill your God dream. Deal with them quickly and get on with building God's kingdom.

THE RESTORATION OF A DREAM
Not only did God save the day but I love the last verse in the chapter. Gen.12:20 (NASB)

"Pharaoh commanded his men concerning him; and they escorted him away, with his wife and all that belonged to him."

When God restores you, He gives you back what belonged to you in the first place. He returns to you all that was lost and sends you on your way to promise. Too many of us sit wondering if God can really help us, or we sit in discouragement because we expect ourselves to be experts in a place we've never been. Give it to God! Ask Him to restore the dream. He can do a miracle even today!

MAIN THOUGHTS TODAY
- Dreams stay with us through success and failure
- Unbelief and fear are dream killers
- The restoration of dreams

TODAY WE LOOKED AT THE DREAM KILLERS, SPECIFICALLY FEAR
AND UNBELIEF. CONSIDER THE POWER OF GOD TO KEEP THE
DREAM ALIVE. HE WILL RESTORE ALL TO YOU EVEN WHEN YOU'RE IN
OVER YOUR HEAD.

QUESTIONS *(Take time to write in your Journal)*

Have you allowed fear or unbelief to take dreams from you?
Explain.

Are there things that need to be restored and given back to
you that you gave away in fear? Take a moment and ask God to
forgive you for coming up with your own plan to save the dream.
Ask Him to do what only He can do: bring full restoration.

Do you have a plan for the next time fear and unbelief try to
come to steal your dream? Try to be as practical as possible.

WRITE OUT YOUR PRAYER HERE (OR IN YOUR JOURNAL)

RUNNING OUT OF TIME

Storyline — *Abram and Sarah were running out of time; they were getting older by the minute. As their dreams got further and further away, God was right on time.*

DREAMS NOT BOUND BY TIME

Abraham and Sarah were not getting any younger. In fact, they had been losing significant time. All those stars seemed as if they had become pieces of sand, slipping through their fingers. Abraham was desperate. He tried everything and now time was expiring.

Dream chasing isn't bound by human standards or earthly time clocks. God is the creator of time. He is not subject to what we think is a normal or an acceptable amount of time. He doesn't always move quickly, but He is always right on time.

THE ENEMY ALWAYS LIES ABOUT TIME

Genuinely, this is the hardest part of holding the dream. It's all fun and games until you are another year older, or you're still childless, broke, or sick. It can shake you. Time feels like the grim reaper coming to call, and you keep avoiding his knock. Until you surrender your timeframe, you won't find peace.

I have found in my own life that dreams can become idols. We can get so focused on fulfilling the dream that we begin to serve the dream rather than the Dream Giver. It's always when

I find myself explaining to God that He's doing it wrong or He's running out of time that I have to check myself. I usually find a quiet place to get on my knees and just surrender to the journey. My rushing God to hurry Him up will do no good. I have to trust Him. He began this work. I love how the Bible says,

"...being confident of this, that he who began a good work in you will carry it on to completion until the day of Christ Jesus."
Philippians 1:6 (NIV)

The enemy will always try to speed you up. He'll try to get you to make quick decisions to change the season. We get in so much trouble when we do this. Call him out like the liar that he is and surrender to God quickly.

THE HAND OF GOD IS SWIFT

Trust me when I say, God moves very quickly. I've seen it over and over in my decades of serving Him. When it's time, He doesn't mess around. Overnight, Sarah was pregnant and on her way to becoming a Mother to the nations. God was faithful to His Word. Don't be surprised that when God says it's time, it will leave your head spinning.

God loves to break in! God loves to display His glory, and one way He does is moving on an expired due date. Remember, if everything were on time it would be hard to say it was the hand of God. The miracle of being close to 100 years old and barren is the stuff great stories of faith make. Let's read about it in Hebrews 11, otherwise known at the Hall of Faith.

HEBREWS 11:8-12 (NIV)

By faith Abraham, when called to go to a place he would later receive as his inheritance, obeyed and went, even though he did not know where he was going. By faith he made his home in the promised land like a stranger in a foreign country; he lived in tents, as did Isaac and Jacob, who were heirs with him of the same promise. For he was looking forward to the city with foundations, whose architect and builder is God. And by faith even Sarah, who was past childbearing age, was enabled to bear children because she considered him faithful who had made the promise. And so from this one man, and he as good as dead, came descendants as numerous as the stars in the sky and as countless as the sand on the seashore.

MAIN THOUGHTS TODAY

- Dreams are not bound by human time
- The enemy always lies about time
- The hand of God is swift

ADD FIVE MINUTES TO YOUR STUDY

TODAY WE LEARNED THAT GOD'S DREAMS FOR OUR LIVES ARE NOT SUBJECT TO HUMAN TIMECLOCKS. THE ENEMY WILL ALSO TRY AND LIE TO YOU ABOUT RUNNING LATE, BUT GOD MOVES QUICKLY AND ON TIME.

Do you feel like you're running out of time for the promises of God in your life? Explain.

Have you heard of the three-day rule? I will give myself three days to fight discouragement, depression, or even anxiety, but after that amount of time I begin to ask myself some hard questions. Where have I believed a lie? Are you at this point in your story? Explain.

When we send the lie away from us and nail it to the cross (simply knowing Jesus took authority of every lie on the cross), the Holy Spirit will replace the lie with the truth. Take a moment and ask Him what truth He's giving you about your timeframe?

WRITE OUT YOUR PRAYER HERE (OR IN YOUR JOURNAL)

SHORTCUTTING THE DREAM

Storyline — Abram and Sarai devise a plan to make the dream happen. It results in heartache, pain, a child, and delay. God's vision will be cut short no matter how long the journey.

THE ENEMY WILL ALWAYS LIE ABOUT A SHORTCUT

Abram and Sarai devise a plan to shortcut God's promise. It's messy from the start. Abram will take Sarai's maidservant Hagar and get her pregnant. Voila'! ... problem solved, or so they thought! A son is born, Ishmael. Sarai sees Hagar is pregnant and immediately has contempt and pain. I often read this passage growing up, but it wasn't until I was married and a Mom did I get it. Once Sarai sees Hagar pregnant, she must have realized she was the problem. She was the one who couldn't get pregnant. I'm sure it confirmed her worst fear.

When we step out of the plan of God, we usually cause unnecessary pain. Not only was Sarai barren, but now she had a servant who was pregnant with her husband's child. I've seen this over and over again in life. When we humans get tired of waiting, we make it happen. We marry the next guy, move to a different city, change jobs, take a debt-filled vacation, etc. Not only does this not hurry the hand of God, but we now have a serious mess on our hands. We will try and act like we didn't do it, but we can't get rid of the consequences.

ISHMAELS ARE REAL

The reality is you can create an Ishmael yourself. God doesn't make us do what He knows is best, so our free will is operating. If we try and fast forward to make a change, we can create a child, but it's not the promise.

I like to say, "You can pick your sin, but you can't choose your consequences." If you come to God repenting and pregnant, you will still be pregnant after the prayer. God doesn't step into every consequence. He allows you to feel the pain. Why? Because he has a system already set up to teach us things; it's called sowing and reaping. God allows us to sow seeds, but once we sow seeds, we can expect to reap a harvest. Now let me say, we don't reap every seed we've sowed. We deserved death, the Bible says, and God made a way for us. God is still as faithful to His promise as He was with Isaac. (Their son ... but we're getting ahead of ourselves.) Ishmael was still alive and his descendants are still here today. Sarai and Abram did nothing for the promise but create more problems and delay.

GOD STILL SEES ISAAC

Unlike most humans, God can see the whole picture. Even when we are busy creating Ishmaels, He's still working on Isaac. I love this thought! It doesn't matter how much of a mess you are cleaning up. It doesn't matter how many Ishmaels you are taking care of; God is still working on the promise. It's going to take fortitude and resolve. You may have to spend some time renewing your mind, as it says in Romans.

"Do not conform to the pattern of this world, but be transformed by the renewing of your mind. Then you will be able to test and approve what God's will is—his good, pleasing and perfect will."
Romans 12:2 (NIV)

You can be transformed, and God can continue to create in you a clean heart (See Psalms 51:10). Many of our heroes in the faith produced Ishmaels, and God made a way. David made a mess with Bathsheba, Eve made a mess with the Apple, Samson with Delilah, etc. Even though they lived with the consequences of their decisions, God made a way and fulfilled His promise.

MAIN THOUGHTS TODAY

- The enemy will try to get you to shortcut
- Ishmaels are real
- God still sees Isaac

ADD FIVE MINUTES TO YOUR STUDY

TODAY WE LEARNED THE HARD TRUTH THAT GOD WILL ALLOW US TO GIVE BIRTH TO ISHMAELS IN OUR LIVES WHEN WE TRY TO SHORTCUT THE PROMISE. BUT EVEN WHEN WE HAVE TO LIVE WITH CONSEQUENCES OF OUR CHOICES, GOD IS STILL AT WORK ON OUR ISAAC.

Have you been tempted to give birth to Ishmaels in your life? Did you try to rush the hand of God and are now living with those choices? Explain.

Part of us growing up and becoming the person who can carry the promise is owning our choices. Are there areas in your life you need to make right? Relationships you need to ask forgiveness? Is there money you need to pay back? Addictions you need to break? Now's the time! Explain.

Are you having a hard time seeing your Isaac because you feel like all you're doing is taking care of your Ishmaels? Ask God to give you a fresh vision. He's been fighting for you even when you don't feel it.

WRITE OUT YOUR PRAYER HERE (OR IN YOUR JOURNAL)

DELAYING THE DREAM

Storyline — God told Abram to leave Ur and live in Canaan, but Abram didn't listen all the way. He took along his father, Terah, whose name meant "delay" and he lived in Haran, a place with a name meaning "barren."

PARTIAL OBEDIENCE LEADS TO DELAY

I love this part of the story. To be honest, it's right at the beginning of the promise, but it holds so much truth I can barely contain myself. We find ourselves in the book of Genesis chapter 11:31–32.

"Terah took his son Abram, his grandson Lot, son of Haran, and his daughter-in-law Sarai, the wife of his son Abram, and together they set out from Ur of the Chaldeans to go to Canaan. But when they came to Haran, they settled there. Terah lived 205 years, and he died in Haran."(NIV)

God spoke to Abram about leaving Ur and going to live in Canaan. Canaan was Abram's Promised Land. But Abram didn't listen all the way. He took his family with him, including his cousin, Lot, and his father, Terah. His father's name meant 'delay.' What an incredible reality!

Partial obedience leads to a delayed promise. It's important we don't believe we have obeyed when we've only listened halfway. Full obedience is Godly obedience. It's the only way not to delay the promise. If God said it, then there must be a reason for it. Trust him!

PARTIAL OBEDIENCE LEADS TO BARRENNESS

Abram took his family and lived in a place with a name meaning 'barren.' When we don't obey God all the way we end up living a barren life. We end up living a dull life. We may think it's not a big deal, but God is trying to lead us to a land flowing with milk and honey. When we wait to obey God, we aren't in a place to bear fruit and live. We are just buying time.

The Bible says we can be like a tree planted by living water. We may not bear fruit in every season, but our leaves will not wither.

Psalms 1:3 (NIV)
That person is like a tree planted by streams of water, which yields its fruit in season and whose leaf does not wither—whatever they do prospers.

GO BACK TO WHAT GOD SAID

What do we do when we find ourselves in a place of partial obedience? We have to go back to the last thing God told us to do. It may seem anticlimactic, but it's the only sure thing to do.

Many times in my life, I have gotten lost in the journey. I've only obeyed enough to feel good about my decision but not enough to say I fully listened to God. I have to go back to what He said to me in the beginning. I go back to the last time He clearly spoke to me and see if I delayed. I then purpose to respond from this moment.

It may not be where I want to go. It may seem like a lot of work, but I'm committed to trusting God. Once Abram obeyed God, he was on his way to his promise. He didn't know God was going to promise him a legacy as vast as the stars. He didn't know he would have the son of his dreams. He only knew he needed to get to Canaan.

God has so much in store for you. Don't let your dream chasing become delayed. Don't let it throw you when it looks like someone is taking the best part of your Promised Land. Even if the dream feels like it's slipping away or you're running out of time, don't buy into fear and unbelief. Go back, and start again. Don't be afraid of your Ishmaels. Keep going! The best is yet to come.

MAIN THOUGHTS TODAY
- Partial obedience leads to delay
- Partial obedience leads to barrenness
- Go back to what God said

ADD FIVE MINUTES TO YOUR STUDY
TODAY WE LEARNED OUR DREAMS AND PROMISES ARE DELAYED WHEN WE CHOOSE ONLY TO OBEY HALFWAY. WE HAVE TO GO BACK TO THE LAST THING GOD ASKED US TO DO. OBEY AND GET ON YOUR WAY!

Is there an area in your life where you see you only obeyed God halfway? Explain.

What is the next thing you can do to go back and start where you left off? Sometimes it's best to have a friend to help keep you accountable when it comes to the hard stuff. Look for someone who loves you, will be honest, and most importantly checks in on what you asked them.

What areas of our study this week spoke to you the most? Explain.

- Losing the Dream
- Dreams Slipping Away
- Running Out Of Time
- Shortcutting the Dream
- Delaying the Dream

WRITE OUT YOUR PRAYER HERE (OR IN YOUR JOURNAL)

DREAM FULFILLED

The Bible says, "A dream fulfilled is a tree of life." (Proverbs 13:12 NLT) There is NOTHING sweeter than watching your promise fulfilled right before your eyes. It leaves you feeling satisfied, established, and confident.

The best simple illustration I can think of has to be a child (it could be because I've had four children, so humor me). It all begins with the moment you receive the news you are pregnant. Your world is left spinning. The thought of you being a parent, or better yet, the thought of a human being growing inside of you, is almost more than your brain can contain. It's exciting and invigorating. You begin to plan and prepare, and then you wait... and you wait. Did I mention you wait? There are doctor's appointments, name choosing, crib building, and birth classes. Your whole focus is to birth this baby and have it be healthy. Finally, almost a year later, you give birth to this baby. It's euphoric! In one moment, all the waiting, the aches and pain of a growing belly, the cost of upgrading your life to make room, becomes irrelevant. The sweetest joy comes when you experience the birth of a promise!

Our spirits are the same way. We can't help ourselves! Words like 'euphoric' and 'irrelevant' come into play. I can't imagine what Abram and Sarah were feeling. When all seemed lost. when all felt expired, they gave birth to a promise.

This week we are going to journey into the land of promise. We're going to explore what it looks like to live with a dream fulfilled. What does it look like to nurture a vision? What does it take to keep the dream alive? Sometimes we are so consumed with having a baby we forget we are going to have to raise the child. Our promise is no different. Once we give birth, we have to cultivate the right environment to not only keep it alive, but thriving.

Genesis 21: 1-8 (MSG)
God visited Sarah exactly as he said he would; God did to Sarah what he promised: Sarah became pregnant and gave Abraham a son in his old age, and at the very time God had set. Abraham named him Isaac. When his son was eight days old, Abraham circumcised him just as God had commanded. Abraham was a hundred years old when his son Isaac was born. Sarah said, God has blessed me with laughter and all who get the news will laugh with me! She also said, Whoever would have suggested to Abraham that Sarah would one day nurse a baby! Yet here I am! I've given the old man a son! The baby grew and was weaned. Abraham threw a big party on the day Isaac was weaned.

NEW LIFE OF A DREAM

Storyline — At last Isaac (the dream) was born when Abraham was 100 years, and Sarah over 90 years of age. God was right on time! The promise was fulfilled just as God had said it would be.

GOD DOES NOT LIE

God does not lie. I love the way Beth Moore reminds us, "God is who He said He is, and He will do what He said He will do." I have personally stood on this promise more times than I can count, and I can imagine Abram, now Abraham, and Sarai, now Sarah, doing the same. It's a core value we must carry until we have the breakthrough.

Mark 10 is one of those scriptures which brings us a lot of clarity.

"Jesus looked at them and said, "With man this is impossible, but not with God; all things are possible with God."
Mark10:27 (NIV)

Better yet, the Message version says,

Jesus was blunt: "No chance at all if you think you can pull it off by yourself. Every chance in the world if you let God do it."
Mark 10:27 (MSG)

GOD'S PROMISES NEVER FAIL
At once, after enough drama for your Mama, we find Sarah is pregnant.

Genesis 21:1 (NIV)
"Now the Lord was gracious to Sarah as he had said, and the Lord did for Sarah what he had promised."

The Bible says, "The Lord did for Sarah what He had promised." This promise took 25 years to accomplish, but God did it. (25 YEARS... Doesn't that make you feel a little better about your life?) God's promises never fail. If you like to underline in your Bible, I would underline or circle the word 'did.' We find this to be true in our lives. When we have a promise fulfilled, we can easily lose sight of the One who made it happen.

Finding a way to keep this in front of you will be very important. You may need to make a visual reminder or have something you say on a regular basis. In my kitchen, I have a visual reminder. It's a little metal picture that says, "I can do all this through Him who gives me strength" (Philippians 4:13). Each time I look at this picture, I'm reassured a little more that every blessing I've experienced and every promise fulfilled is because He gave me the strength to see it through.

THE DIFFERENCE BETWEEN A PROMISE
Some promises of God are conditional with what He asked us to do, and some are dependent on something He said He would do. Sarah and Abraham's promise was dependent on what God said He would do, not on anything they needed to do. Abraham didn't obey God perfectly, but God was faithful to do what He said He would do.

If you're sitting in a fulfilled promise, you are here for one of two reasons. You did what God asked you to do, or God said it and it was as good as done. Regardless of why you are here, enjoy! It's a time for celebration. Look back and see how far you have come. Enjoy the season; it's unlike any you've been in before.

DREAMS HOLD LEGACY

The only way to truly leave a lasting legacy is to live as a Dream Chaser. We can't forget our dream is always connected to the big dream of God. God's dream is for the family. It's for lasting fruit, and He wants our story to be connected to His GREAT story. Having a dream fulfilled is confirmation you are living out your God-given legacy. It's deeply fulfilling because it's deeply Kingdom.

MAIN THOUGHTS TODAY

- God does not lie
- God's Promises Never Fail
- The Difference Between a Promises
- Dreams Hold Legacy

ADD FIVE MINUTES TO YOUR STUDY

TODAY WE REFLECTED ON THE TRUTH THAT GOD DOES NOT LIE AND HIS PROMISES NEVER FAIL. WE CAN TRUST THAT A PROMISED FULFILLED IS A LEGACY CREATED.

How does it make you feel when you read the phrase, "God is who He says He is, and He will do what He said He will do?" Explain.

Are you in a season of fulfillment? What visual reminder have you prepared to help you stay connected to God's strength in your life? Explain.

Knowing the difference between the promise being dependent or conditional, what was/is your journey? Explain.

WRITE OUT YOUR PRAYER HERE (OR IN YOUR JOURNAL)

PROTECTING A DREAM

Storyline — Now that the dream is born, your primary job is to keep it safe and make sure it thrives to live. This season is unique; it requires focus, protection, nurture and health.

Ecclesiastes 3:1-8 (AMP)
There is a season (a time appointed) for everything and a time for every delight and event or purpose under heaven—
A time to be born and a time to die;
A time to plant and a time to uproot what is planted.
A time to kill and a time to heal;
A time to tear down and a time to build up.
A time to weep and a time to laugh;
A time to mourn and a time to dance.
A time to throw away stones and a time to gather stones;
A time to embrace and a time to refrain from embracing.
A time to search and a time to give up as lost;
A time to keep and a time to throw away.
A time to tear apart and a time to sew together;
A time to keep silent and a time t
A time for war and a time for peace.

DREAMS MUST BE PROTECTED

Once a promise is fulfilled, the environment we keep it in will be vital to the health of its development. We want to live in the Promise Land. I think this is where many of us lack understanding. The journey isn't over; it's just beginning. Learning to live in this new environment requires stewardship.

1 Corinthians 9:17 (AMP)
For if I do this work of my own free will, then I have a reward; but if it is not of my will [but by God's choosing], I have been entrusted with a [sacred] stewardship.

Three of our four sons were born in the winter. When we prepared to take them home from the hospital, we were told to be very careful. Winter was a season where people get the flu, and if our son got sick, he would have to return to the hospital. They urged us to please protect his little body.

Dreams are the same way. When we have them born in our lives, they are new and fresh, but fragile. We are just getting used to living with this new truth, and we must protect it.

DREAMS REQUIRE A HEALTHY ENVIRONMENT
Part of stewardship is protecting. The environment you create around your fulfilled dream will be necessary.

The doctors used this phrase all the time with our infants. We need them to 'Thrive to Live.' What this meant was the fragility of this new life required the environment not just to be 'good enough' but to be a 'climate to thrive.' It was the only way to ensure essential health and vitality.

So what does this mean practically? What you listen to on a daily basis, read, hang around, or consume needs to be healthy. If you are trying to live as a newly married woman and all you do is read about the dating life, hang out with single women and watch shows glamorizing single women, you aren't setting a 'thrive to live' environment.

Let's say you've just had a promise fulfilled of getting your dream job. The best thing you can do is get a life coach or someone to help you adjust, read books on the position, and try to connect with those who have done this before. Sitting back and thinking, "I've got this... now I can go on autopilot," will jeopardize your full promise. You are responsible for your environment, so go for it. Do what you need to do.

DREAMS HAVE SEASONS

You won't be in this season forever. You will gradually be able to relax, confidently aware of your surroundings. Eventually, you're going to be able to live out this promise no matter if the environment is 'thrive to live' or 'just ok' (See Ecclesiastes 3:1-8).

Remember how we talked about my journey to discovering my call to influence? I explained I was a 'natural convincer' but I didn't have all the gifts to become a voice of influence. When I began, the Lord gave me a promise that this was on my life. I started to believe and watched the promised start to unfold. I was now a voice and a leader of people (even with Mr. Microphone... wink), but I lacked confidence, clarity, and wisdom. I had to care for the dream. I positioned myself in environments where I could learn. I made sure to have friends around me who were cheering me on and knew my heart even if my words didn't always match up. I listened to books, received prayer, accepted counsel, and monitored my community. I began to grow not just as a leader, but as a person, and eventually I grew in confidence. I knew that no matter where God placed me, I would be ok. I was grounded in the promise, and I wasn't going anywhere.

MAIN THOUGHTS TODAY

- Dreams must be protected
- Dreams require a healthy environment
- Dreams have seasons

ADD FIVE MINUTES TO YOUR STUDY

TODAY WE LEARNED THAT IN ORDER FOR DREAMS TO THRIVE, THEY NEED TO BE GUARDED AND NURTURED. DREAMS HAVE SEASONS, AND THEY WILL NOT ALWAYS NEED TO LIVE IN SUCH A PROTECTED SEASON.

What environment have you set up to make sure your dreams Thrive to Live? Is there something you've invested in to make sure they stay alive? Explain.

Are there changes you need to ensure their health? What can you do today to give them a quality environment? Explain.

Are you clear on the season of your promise? Take some time to ask the Lord where you are in the journey. He would love to tell you and infuse you with strength, so just ask.

WRITE OUT YOUR PRAYER HERE (OR IN YOUR JOURNAL)

Storyline — God will put you in a community of dreamers: people who support the dream even if it takes a while for it to happen. He will surround you with a unique tribe of God-following, dream-chasing, stargazing, Promised Land dwellers.

COMMUNITY OF DREAMERS

The Bible is very clear that we need each other. The family is God's idea. Think about it... the fact is, we aren't just dropped off by the stork (Please ask your Mom if you're not sure what this means... wink), but God's original design was to have a man and woman come together to make a child. He wanted every child to be born with a Father and a Mother in a family unit. Our stories don't always fall into place, but God made a way for each of us to get what we need even if we don't have all the elements. He designed us to need spiritual fathers, mothers, sisters, and brothers; a spiritual family. He was confident we would grow the healthiest and happiest in a community. I love how Hebrews puts it.

Hebrews 10:24-25 (AMP)
"...and let us consider [thoughtfully] how we may encourage one another to love and to do good deeds, not forsaking our meeting together [as believers for worship and instruction], as is the habit of some, but encouraging one another; and all the more [faithfully] as you see the day [of Christ's return] approaching."

God wants you to have a beautiful community, and He wishes to help you build it. He is very invested in this thought. His desire is for us to help bear each other's burdens (Galatians 6:2). He knew we would be better together, and two were better than one (Ecclesiastes 4:9).

In fact, He gave us the promise that when two of us get together in His name, He will be there (Matthew 18:20). What motivation!

We also want to look at this from the Dream Chasing angle. Living with intention and purpose will draw people with likeminded lives. The healthier you are, the healthier your community will be because you will have healthy boundaries and only allow those behaving nicely to be around you.

SEASONAL TRIBE

In the Bible, we see God placing groups of people into tribes. These were their 'people.' There are a lot of reasons God chose tribes that we won't get into right now, but I love the word tribe, and I'm going to use it today to help you understand this principle.

God will give us a tribe that's for life. My family easily fits into this category. They loved me and invested in me from the beginning of my life. I was born into their tribe, if you will. I belong to them, they belong to me, and because they love the Lord, we can encourage each other in the things of God. I now have some lifetime friends that fit into this category as well. We have been with each other through thick and thin. We are in it for life. They are my Life Tribe.

Other times, God will place you in a tribe for a season. Something you have and something they have clicks, and you begin to encourage each other. It's a special time, and it leaves you wondering if these people will become your Life Tribe, but eventually things change. If we don't realize that's okay, and we didn't do anything wrong, we will hold on too long. They are our Seasonal Tribe. God placed them in our lives for the season at hand. It was what you needed, it was what they needed, but time has shifted. It's best to know when the season has changed, thank God for the time, and keep Dream Chasing. Don't get stuck trying to make something work, holding on to something that isn't the right thing anymore. Let it go! You have your Life Tribe.

Note: Sometimes it takes a lot of time to build your tribe, so give yourself grace. You may be an entirely different person than you were a year ago and that means your tribe has completely shifted. The worst thing we can do is get overwhelmed trying to make something happen or become exclusive in fear we'll lose them if we include anyone else. Trust God with your story and your relationships.

PROMISED LAND DWELLERS
Lastly, it's important we know who we are running alongside. I love the phrase, "If you're the smartest person in the room, you're in the wrong room." I compare it to Dream Chasing. If you're the only one Dream Chasing in your tribe, you might be working harder than you need to. You're looking for a particular people who want to live in the Promised Land. You're not searching for those satisfied with settling for Ishmaels; you're searching for those willing to wait for Isaac.

MAIN THOUGHTS TODAY
- Community of Dreamers
- Seasonal Tribe
- Promised Land dwellers

ADD FIVE MINUTES TO YOUR STUDY
TODAY WE LEARNED GOD WORKS IN FAMILY AND OUR TRIBE IS VITAL. GOD GIVES US A LIFE TRIBE AND SEASONAL TRIBES. LOOKING FOR DREAM CHASERS IN OUR RELATIONSHIPS IS SIGNIFICANT TO BEING A DREAMER.

Take a moment and note your community. Write two lists, one for your Life Tribe and the other for your Seasonal Tribe.

If you would like God to add more relationships to your life, ask Him to do so. What can you do in the next season to cultivate healthy relationships around you? Explain.

Are you grateful for your tribe? Have you been given a group of healthy relationships? Most importantly, thank God for what He's given you. Take a moment to write down a note on how grateful you are.

WRITE OUT YOUR PRAYER HERE (OR IN YOUR JOURNAL)

AUTHENTICATING A DREAM

Storyline — God had one final test for Abraham. He wanted to know that Isaac was truly His. God will test us even after the dream is real. He intends to know if we have the character to hold the promise and the leadership to steward it well.

THE ISAAC TEST

After the dream is fulfilled for Abraham and Sarah, life seems to go on as normal. Isaac is growing up as the promised son, the delight of their lives, the miracle child, until we hit a screeching halt in Genesis 22 that leaves us all spinning. If you would like to read the whole thing (and I highly recommend it), you can read all 19 verses.

The Reader's Digest version goes like this: God instructs Abraham to get up in the morning and go to the region of Moriah. He says this,

"Take your son, your only son, whom you love—Isaac—and go to the region of Moriah. Sacrifice him there as a burnt offering on a mountain I will show you."
Genesis 22:2

It's hard not to miss the words "your only son" and "whom you love." It's almost like God wanted us to know Abraham hadn't lost any crazy love for his son. He was smitten.

Abraham obeys God and gets up the next morning, taking his son and two servants with him. Abraham doesn't delay. On the journey there, Isaac asks his father a question.

Isaac spoke up and said to his father Abraham, "Father?"

"Yes, my son?" Abraham replied.

"The fire and wood are here," Isaac said, "but where is the lamb for the burnt offering?"

Abraham answered, "God himself will provide the lamb for the burnt offering, my son." And the two of them went on together. (Genesis 22:7-8)

I can't imagine how Abraham was feeling at this moment. I believe he was hoping God would provide a different sacrifice. But let's not forget God had built Abraham year by year, season by season, from being a man WITH faith to a man OF faith.

Let's take a breather for a minute and reflect. What God has done in you, and all the things you've gone through to see your promise fulfilled were not and are not in vain. He was making you the person who could have the character to hold the promise. Part of a seemingly delayed promise is not a God who has forgotten but a God who graciously grants us time to surrender. God had walked Abraham through giving away his land, his years, his son, Ishmael, and now He was asking for Isaac. God had been preparing him.

Abraham takes Isaac with him and leaves the two other men behind telling them they would return. We don't know if he thought God would change His mind or raise Isaac from the dead but, regardless, he was still hoping they would both come back.

Eventually, he builds an altar and Isaac, who is now old enough to understand (scholars believed he was around 30 years of age), would agree to climb up on it to be sacrificed. The type of Biblical sacrifice was that Abraham would kill him and then burn his body. Abraham raises his knife to obey God and kill his son when the angel of God stopped him right in his tracks.

But the angel of the Lord called out to him from heaven, "Abraham! Abraham!"

"Here I am," he replied.

"Do not lay a hand on the boy," he said. "Do not do anything to him. Now I know that you fear God, because you have not withheld from me your son, your only son." (Genesis 22:11-12)

God spares Isaac (and we all take a collective sigh of relief). Abraham obeyed God till the end. We learned a few things that God was looking for in the stewardship of the promise.

God wants to know that what He gives us is still His, and we are simply stewarding the promise. It's critical we understand this principle. The moment we try to claim or own what God has given us is the moment we can lose our commitment to fully obeying God. We will be tested along the way (Don't worry... God will NEVER ask you to harm anything in your life. Only the Devil would ask you to hurt someone in the name of God). Our best defense is to keep surrendering and honoring what God has given us, continuing to hold the promise fulfilled with honor. If we can stay humble, we will be safe, the Bible says.

But he gives more grace. Therefore it says, "God opposes the proud, but gives grace to the humble." James 4:6 (ESV)

MAIN THOUGHTS TODAY
- The Isaac Test (Obedience)

ADD FIVE MINUTES TO YOUR STUDY
TODAY WE LEARNED ABOUT THE TEST WE WILL HAVE TO GO THROUGH EVEN AFTER A PROMISE FULFILLED. OUR BEST DEFENSE IS TO STEWARD THE GIFT BY STAYING HUMBLE AND OBEYING QUICKLY.

QUESTIONS *(Take time to write in your Journal)*

After reading our text today, what was the one thing that stood out to you about the Isaac Test? Explain.

Do you have a hard time not taking ownership of the promise God has given you? What is something you can do today to communicate stewardship? Explain.

Humility isn't a personality; it's a perspective and a heart attitude. Take some time today to write out James 4:6 and put it to memory.

WRITE OUT YOUR PRAYER HERE (OR IN YOUR JOURNAL)

Storyline — Dreaming with God is a part of your life in God. God communicates to us through dreams, and we will live out many dreams throughout our lives. What's most important is that we continue to do it all in the name of Jesus.

DREAMING WITH GOD IS LIFE IN GOD

Our God-induced ability to dream with Him, the One who made the Heavens and the Earth, is still one of the greatest mysteries to unfold. When we're in our healthiest and Godliest place, dreaming with Him should be natural. Vision and purpose come together and give us our birthright. Partnering with God is our only fulfilling lifestyle. It's the way we best know Him. He wants to interact with us and get right in the middle.

"I am the Good Shepherd, and I know [without any doubt those who are] My own and My own know Me [and have a deep, personal relationship with Me]"
John 10:14 (AMP)

God wants to be known, and He continues year after year, time after time, generation after generation, to make Himself known.

Dreaming with God is life in God. It will take years for some dreams to come true and for others it will take a lifetime. Still other dreams will morph into dreams you never knew you had, but they were what you needed all along. Dreaming with God is meant to enhance your relationship with Him. God desires to keep us dependent, all the while full of hope. Your history of dreaming with God will build a deeper and deeper well. God moments that will ground you and make you a person not WITH faith but OF faith. It's life in God!

GOD WILL GIVE YOU MANY DREAMS

God will continue to give you many dreams because He has many dreams for you. He can't stop dreaming about your life even when you have stopped dreaming for yourself. The moment you plug back into the power of God, you will experience God's desire to dream for your life again. Jeremiah is one of those verses we all need in our lives on a regular basis.

For I know the plans I have for you," declares the Lord, "plans to prosper you and not to harm you, plans to give you hope and a future.
Jeremiah 29:11 (NIV)

I love how the Message paraphrases it:

"I know what I'm doing. I have it all planned out—plans to take care of you, not abandon you, plans to give you the future you hope for."
Jeremiah 29:11 (MESS)

He knows what He's doing more than we ever will. He's not going to abandon us. He has plans (dreams) to give us a future, and with the vision of our future.

FULFILLED DREAMS ARE A FULFILLED LIFE

The reason we have such a desire and drive to see our visions come true is because God places within them deep fulfillment. He knew the moment we partnered to see our desire accomplished that we would be invested entirely in the dream. Dreams fulfilled leave us deeply satisfied and more connected to Him than before.

Hope deferred makes the heart sick,
But when desire is fulfilled, it is a tree of life.
Proverbs 13:12 (AMP)

I believe the Bible is telling us a desire (dream) fulfilled, is a vibrant life.

EAT PRAY HUSTLE
At the end of the day, life in God is practical, and it's spiritual. It's living as a dream chasing, Jesus following, hope-filled, stargazer. Some days living out the vision of God for your life is going to be exciting and full of possibilities and other days it's going to seem mundane and uneventful. The journey isn't always in the fulfillment but in the chasing that keeps us fully alive. We are always looking for God.

This study has been about learning to Dream Chase with God. No more wondering if God has a plan or if you can accomplish your purpose. It's clear! Don't live another moment on the sidelines. Jump in and begin. The dream is alive... go after it!

MAIN THOUGHTS TODAY
- Dreaming with God is life in God
- God will give you many dreams
- Fulfilled dreams is a fulfilled life

ADD FIVE MINUTES TO YOUR STUDY
TODAY WE LEARNED DREAMING WITH GOD IS LIFE IN GOD. THE MORE FULFILLED DREAMS WE HAVE, THE MORE FULFILLED LIFE WE EXPERIENCE.

What is the one thing that you felt God was speaking to you about during this study? If you were to put it in one sentence what would it be? Explain.

Take some time to write down your dreams. Ask yourself what a fulfilled dream would look like at the end of the season? Explain.

Is there someone in your life who needs this study? Take a moment to write their name down and make a point this week to let them in on it.

WRITE OUT YOUR PRAYER HERE (OR IN YOUR JOURNAL)

HAVILAH'S RESOURCES

STUDIES / DEVOTIONALS

I Do Hard Things

Radical Growth

The Good Stuff

TEACHINGS

Becoming a Voice

Free Your Mind

Annointed & Qualified

Find these and other great resources at
havilahcunnington.com

STAY CONNECTED

website *havilahcunnington.com*

facebook *Havilah Cunnington*

twitter *@mrshavilah*

instagram *havilahcunnington*

youtube *youtube.com/user/havilahcunnington*

email *info@havilahcunnington.com*

FOR MORE INFORMATION
email info@havilahcunnington.com

join our newsletter

REQUEST HAVILAH TO SPEAK

WOMEN **+** STUDENTS **+** CHURCHES

FOR
*Retreats, conferences, one-night gatherings,
church services, leadership events*

Made in the USA
Middletown, DE
16 February 2019